Jesus the Christ
Greatest Rapper of All Time

A Guide to Evangelizing Hip Hop Culture

Ricardo Palmer

Jesus the Christ, Greatest Rapper of All Time
A Guide to Evangelizing Hip Hop Culture

Printed in the United States of America

Cover design by Derrick M. Davis for Think Distorted Creative Design Group

ISBN 978-0-615-35373-9

DEDICATION

To the women in my life.

*My loving wife, Christine, who actually deserves the title of coauthor.
Your commitment and dedication has been the backbone of this
project.*

*My mother, Richardine Jackson, who interceded for my soul when I
had gone astray.
You welcomed me back with open arms of love and encouragement.*

*My grandmother, Carrie Belle Palmer, for being rooted in the Lord
and
raising an offspring of God-fearing children.*

*My sister, Tammy Palmer, whose dreams and ambitions far exceeded
my very own
but ignited faith in me that all things are truly possible.*

*My aunt, Sandy Green, who did it first.
Thank you for setting an awesome example.*

CONTENTS

Acknowledgements   *vii*

Explanation of Title   *ix*

Intro   **1**

Chapter 1   **9**
Real Rappers or Real Killers, Dying to Know the Difference

Chapter 2   **15**
Tupac Shakur, Jesus of the Streets

Chapter 3   **37**
Kanye West: Should "Jesus Walk" in Our Church?

Chapter 4   **55**
Well Talk: Creating Dialogue in the Hip Hop Community

Chapter 5   **67**
Paying Caesar: Honoring the King to Gain Access to His People

Chapter 6   **71**
King David, the First Rap Star: Ties Between David and Hip Hop

Chapter 7   **79**
Looking for Legion, Bringing Our Heaven to Their Hell

Chapter 8   **83**
Goliath, the Giant Slave: Making Hip Hop Serve Us

Chapter 9   89
Connected, but Not Married to Hip Hop Culture

Chapter 10   97
Our Wisdom, Their Strength: Helping Our Youth Win Their War

Chapter 11   109
What is "The Truth Behind Hip Hop?"
Addressing the Controversial DVD

Chapter 12   119
Love, But No Love Songs

Out   123

Notes   *126*

ACKNOWLEDGEMENTS

My Lord Jesus Christ – for trusting me with the vision, imparting the revelation, and enabling me to bring it to completion.

Shane Richardson and Tahashi McAllister – for inspiring me and never doubting the plans that God has for me. Everything that the Lord promised shall come to pass.

My dad, John Jackson – for being a provider and protector for the family and for your perseverance and strength through the years.

The entire Palmer family – for your love, acceptance, and support throughout all the seasons of my life.

Pastor Marcus R. Shiver and his wife, Shenitha – for pushing me beyond my strengths and helping me to realize the significance of a spiritual father.

Pastor Donnie Chambers and his wife, Onetha – for your unconditional support and willingness to create opportunities for me to share what God has given me.

The late Pastor Willie Thomas and his wife, LaShawn – for giving me the opportunity to serve and develop my gifts for ministry.

Spirit of Truth Christian Church members, especially my youth – for your encouragement and prayers.

Joy McLaughlin, Hanford Scott, Jerode Davis, Darryl Boyles, Kiosha Gregg and **the young ladies of Kingdom Glory at Columbia College.**

Mrs. Julie Morales and family – for your love and faithfulness.

My mother-in-law, Eliane Cotsford – for your prayers and understanding.

Ben Renrick, John Anderson, Chip Walker, and **Delbert Townsend.**

Additional thanks goes to **Derrick Davis** for the cover design and **Mrs. Patricia Clayton** for the editing.

JESUS CHRIST, A RAPPER?
EXPLANATION OF THE TITLE

When man lost all reverence and respect for God, creating distance and worshipping false idols, it was clear that God had to intervene. God did the one thing that was absolutely unfitting for the Creator to do – He became a man. God became flesh and blood. He became sin in order to bring man back to Himself. Jesus entered man's world as a friend and a brother to usher them back into a true relationship with the Father.

So how can I claim that Jesus is the greatest rapper of all time? Some may consider this sacrilegious. However, Jesus "becomes" a rapper for the same reason that God became a man. We're talking to Hip Hop, a culture that lacks a true understanding of God. This culture anoints American idols and musical icons as their spiritual leaders. To be Hip Hop's greatest rapper is to be their god. Rappers dictate and direct millions of impressionable youth with their hypnotic lyrics and flashy lifestyles. Jesus is seeking to take back the stage and grab the mic in order to reclaim their worship. If we would allow Him, Jesus would like to rap to hip hop culture.

INTRO

The date was December 13, 1996, approximately 9:30 at night. We were at the barbershop, and my partner Tahashi had called home. His mom told him that detectives had come looking for him. Cutting the barbershop trip short, the four of us hopped into the car I was driving, quickly lit up a blunt, and turned the music up, hoping that the clouds of marijuana smoke would literally hide us from the trouble which lay ahead. We were suspected of bank robbery and in a bit of a rush to get out of town; this last bit of information put us in even more of a hurry. I had been questioned earlier in the week by detectives, but they didn't have the evidence that they thought would be enough to lock me up. We knew that they were closing in on us, but looking back, it seems as though we just didn't care. We had robbed yet another bank earlier that day and were headed down I-26 in Columbia, S.C. en route to Atlanta, Georgia. We rapped along with Tupac's "Hail Mary," one of our many theme songs, as we were suddenly interrupted by a flood of police cars. The high-speed chase began, and when it ended, I was facing 30 years in prison. I've forgotten many of the events that accompanied that horrendous night, but that song has always remained fixed in my memory. I sometimes cringe when I hear it in passing. Although the song is called "Hail Mary," it has little to do with honoring Mary, the mother of Jesus. In fact, by that time, I can only remember having considered God a few times in my life. Once was when I had gotten so drunk that I thought I was dying. The other was when I had gotten in trouble for breaking into cars, praying to God that I wouldn't go to jail. In both cases, I had turned towards God only because things were looking pretty bad in my life. Sitting in my jail cell, I found myself with another opportunity to consider God – this time was catastrophic in comparison to the others. At 19 years of age, I was in jail. I had seen all the movies and had the normal fears that anyone else would have. After the initial shock of being arrested, time eventually became time, and sadly enough, I adjusted just fine. My first year and a half was spent in the county jail, which is where guys wait before they are sentenced. I had a $325,000 bond and little hopes of going anywhere. Besides the fighting and the noise, which is so constant it stops being a distraction, all I had was my sober mind questioning everything that I had done in my life. Most guys sleep, watch television, or write love letters. In the county jail, writing a love letter is a serious craft – a brother can get really creative with a pack of Skittles and some toilet tissue! I had no stress relief at all, and to make it worse, there was no music. The only music we heard was on shows like *Apollo* and *Soul Train*. We loved those shows and gathered around the television with religious fervor. You want to see a fight? Stand in a man's way when Soul Train is on the air! Not being able to hear music hurt me to my core because I had always been around it. Earlier, in the summertime, I would help my uncle Kenny who was a D.J.

2

carry crates to functions. My partners in high school were in a hip hop group (everybody had one of those at the time), and I would spend hours listening to music and watching them put tracks together. Music was in me – it drove me; it pushed me; it kept me in rhythm and gave me something to talk about. This was the field in which I was an expert. 'Who is the greatest of all time? Was it Rakim or Biggie? Tupac or Nas?' This was our early morning discussion every other day in high school. We studied rappers' metaphors, similes and rhyme schemes while other students studied Shakespeare. When a hot CD would come out, we would wait in line at midnight in the music store parking lot just to be the first one on the block to have it. I was indifferent to everything else in life except music – it was one of the only things that mattered to me. Now I was locked away from the very first thing that I knew I had a love for. We made our own compositions while in the county jail though, gathering at the end of the hall making beats with our mouths, our hands, and banging on the walls. Anything that created a sound, we'd hit. The older guys hated to see us coming because they knew that we were going to make wild and rambunctious noises until the correction officer broke it up. They were trying to do their time as quietly as possible. We, on the other hand, were doing ours cussing, screaming, kicking, fighting, and above everything else, rapping. I had a roommate who had memorized volumes of Tupac's hits, and he would recite them upon request for hours on end. This was the anecdote for us – we had to deal with our pain the only way we knew.

After my sentencing, I moved away from the county jail and was sent to a state prison. This meant a little more freedom and recreation, but most importantly, it meant that I could purchase a walkman! In prison, a good walkman is like a luxury sedan. You would see headphones that had more miles on them than a long distance 18-wheeler. They would be patched up, taped up, and stitched to hold the necessities in place. No matter its condition, a walkman would never be thrown away. Brothers could bring healing to a walkman! There's no such thing as one that couldn't make music. Music was so vital to us – it was a lifeline, something that penetrated the metal and interrupted the monotony of prison. Music was something that came and unlocked every door and every cell and allowed us to roam freely, just for a little while. That favorite song would come on and guys playing basketball, volleyball, throwing horseshoes or just gathering in small circles would suddenly seem as if they had just received a get out of jail free card! Everybody, without knowing it, would begin to fantasize and daydream, moving in one accord as if they were puppets connected to the same string. Hip hop music was the string that connected us all. In January of 2000, after about three years in, I got saved, receiving Jesus as my Lord and Savior. I made the decision that I would no longer be entertained by music that fed into my corrupt nature; I was now a changed man. I had to cut those strings from myself.

Of all the ways in which God could have created a world, He simply spoke it into existence. In the same way, I wanted to speak life into my world, but I realized that many of my favorite artists did not. I really struggled with this. After listening to great preachers with amazing sermons, I still found myself going back to my bunk and listening to hours of Tupac. Although I would feel so convicted because a lot of what Tupac was saying was contrary to the word of God, I still seemed to relate to him. It was like trying to follow two leaders who were going in different directions. There was no compromise between the two. Hip hop had gotten me through to this point, and now God was taking the helm, promising me a land that flows of milk and honey. I struggled with this until, one day, my walkman broke. I took it the local "walkman technician" (probably the richest man on the prison yard), and he took so long to fix my tunes that I just didn't worry myself about it any longer. The ease with which I let it go of this music is what really let me know that something extraordinary was happening to me. I ended up taking about a year hiatus from all music and completely immersed myself into the word of God. This turned out to be the best time of my young life. All I wanted to do was read my Bible! It consumed everything that was going on around me. I had become a monk – so amazed and in awe of God's Word that I did not want to do anything but read and pray. I barely even came out of my room; the only thing that made me move was the mention of a church service. Later, when I came back to listening to music, I gave gospel music a try. I understood the importance of gospel music, and I did enjoy it, but I still felt somewhat unfulfilled and related more to the hip hop artist. Even when I would read and study Bible characters – Jesus, the disciples, the prophets, David, Solomon – I would relate them to Hip Hop. Sure, I was hearing about heaven in gospel music, but my question was always, 'What hell, specifically, did you go through to get there?' I wanted gospel music to show me the steps it took to get to heaven and at the same time, give me a beat that my grandmother couldn't dance to! I know that we're both saved, but she's 70 and I'm in my twenties. Should we be asked to enjoy the same style of music all the time? A bigger question for me was how could I get the guys around me to go where I was going? This was not only my question; it became my burden. I knew that the answer would have to come through music. Afterall, our favorite rappers, in many ways, were our leaders. They established our trends, influenced our language, and shaped our worldviews. Our world was raw, gritty, and confrontational, and gospel music just didn't speak that language. I needed something to bridge the gap between what I was (which represented most of the guys with whom I was in prison) and who I was becoming. Back then, I did not know that there was such a thing as a Christian rapper.

This was the beginning of my passion to save a hip hop generation. This book really has less to do with rap and more to do with our efforts to evangelize a dying culture that relates and adheres to rap music. Many of us still feel that there is no place for rap in or around the church. Some want to use it but are afraid, not knowing where to draw the line and fearing that it may get out of control. Then there are those of the opposite extreme who put a Jesus sticker on a hip hop party that has not been approved nor inspired by the Holy Spirit. This book will deal with several different groups within the Christian church perspective. When I say hip hop culture, I'm speaking of the star basketball player who's adorned with corn rows, tattoos and platinum chains, the forty-something business executive who wears Sean John business suits, the little girl who does all the latest dances in a pair of Apple Bottom jeans, and the young brother doing time for hustling a few rocks. The world of Hip Hop is expansive and includes those lifestyles and more.

In writing this book, I often referenced my own personal testimonies of spending time in prison, my close connection to the streets, and my involvement in prison and youth ministry. This book addresses the starting point for a person's path to salvation. This is ministry for Hip Hop fresh off the block – on its way to the next party or just in the mall searching for the latest designer jeans. This book will help us to intentionally "get in their lane" as we attempt to redirect them. The questions at hand are:

- How do we address Hip Hop on a national scale as a body of believers?
- What is our responsibility to them as the local church?
- How do we as individuals create openings through conversation and interaction?
- How do we rap to hip hop culture?

****A note to the reader:*

In the following chapters, there are many references to songs by various artists. The lyrics were not included due to copyright restrictions; however, every effort has been made to paraphrase these lyrics in order to make the song's intent clear. The reader is encouraged to research the actual song lyrics by each particular artist, understanding that many of the songs contain explicit and profane language.

Chapter One

REAL RAPPERS OR REAL KILLERS, DYING TO KNOW
THE DIFFERENCE

When my wife Christine and I were still engaged, we went to a seminar that addressed some of the negative effects of hip hop music. Present in the room was a mix of parents, kids, disc-jockeys, rappers and other adults. The panel discussed the usual problems society has with Hip Hop – the sex, language, violence, drug and gun play, etc. After listening for a while, I posed the question, "What do we do with our youth who have trouble distinguishing what's real from what's fake in the world of hip hop music and imagery?" For me, this is the real issue. The truth is that, when Biggie and Tupac (two of Hip Hop's superstars) both got shot with *real* bullets and several rap artists are behind *real* bars, it's difficult for many youth to make the distinction between what is entertainment and what is real life. In 50 Cent's movie *Get Rich or Die Tryin'*, he meets a girlfriend that he hadn't seen in years. She asks him what he does for a living, and he replies, "I'm a gangster." He then laughs and says, "I'm a rapper." Laughing some more, he ends with, "I'm a gangster rapper."[1] Although this was a scene from his movie, 50 Cent and other rappers, along with their audiences, have this same problem of trying to define which of the two they represent. Gangster, rapper, or both? Why is the distinction so difficult?

First of all, rappers who used to be on the streets and involved in the drug game do not rap in past tense. Those who were street hustlers several years ago give the impression that they still hustle illegally on the corner. Their audiences, young and impressionable, equate their perceived success to illegal street activity. However, many of these guys haven't been on the block hustling drugs in ten, 15, or 20 years. I robbed a bank in 1996. That's my testimony, not my lifestyle. When I tell the story, it is a part of my history, not my present. Several of today's artists are older men glorifying what they did in 1988 as if it happened yesterday. When was the last time Snoop Doggy Dogg was in a shootout? Today, he flaunts his blue rag (gang paraphernalia) around Hollywood as if he's in the same line of fire as the gangbanger in Compton, California. Snoop promotes gang activity through his lyrics, but his children won't ever have to see the inside of a failing public school! Lil Wayne has been an entertainer, not a gangbanger, since he was a teenager. Jay-Z is a prime example of an artist who speaks of yesterday's glory of hustling as if it's today's struggle. Keep in mind that, although he did do time in prison years ago for trafficking drugs, today Jay-Z owns Def Jam records, has a successful clothing line, is the owner of the 40/40 Club, and even has part ownership of the basketball franchise, the New Jersey Nets. In his song "Dirt Off Your Shoulders," he makes allusions to cooking up crack cocaine in hopes of producing a nice watch and even attempting to stretch the product out enough so that he's able to purchase a Range or Land Rover from his profits. He doesn't say that this was what he had done years ago when he was a hustler; he speaks as if he is still grinding on the block at this time. This song was on his CD *The Black Album* which was released in 2003. So the streets (and our children more specifically) mistakenly attribute his current success to illegal hustling as opposed to the hard work he has put in as a business entrepreneur.

The Lost Art of Storytelling

Another reason why we and our children struggle with distinguishing what is real and what is fake in Hip Hop is that the art of storytelling has become a lost craft. One of Hip Hop's pioneers, Slick Rick, has a rap called "Children's Story." He writes it almost as if it were a fairy tale, even using the famous opening line "Once upon a time..." In it, he tells the story of a young boy who gets caught up in doing a crime and one bad decision he makes leads to another. He starts with a robbing spree in which he is chased by the police, has a shootout with them, and even holds a woman hostage. In the end, the boy is shot and captured by the police. Slick Rick doesn't give his audience any reason to believe that this story is inspired by his own life experiences. Could you imagine if that song was a hit today? It would be written in first person and would say, 'I robbed the store; *I* held the women hostage; and *I* was chased by the police.' It is no longer enough to simply report on what may be happening in the streets. A legitimate rapper has to become an active participant, not just a spectator. Hip hop culture no longer esteems the role of a reporter or onlooker. Sadly, today our youth actually envy and desire the role of the true-to-life street thug.

Keeping It Real

Rap has always had a longing desire to be as authentic as possible. Sure, it does exaggerate, but it has always boasted that the music and its participants represent what's *really* going on in the hood, the real struggle of inner city street culture. There will always be a divide between the purist of the street who says, 'Keep it real – if you haven't lived it, then don't rap about it,' and those who rap just for the sake of entertaining or making money. As a hip hop audience, we were taught early on to be on the watch for fake M.C.'s, or rappers who do not live their music. Hip hop music persecutes pretenders, setting it apart from any other form of entertainment. No other genre of music pressures its entertainers to actually be and do every word that's uttered or spoken. Consider how detrimental this becomes when rappers consistently talk of hustling, prison, sex, and drugs. What does it mean to be "real" in this culture when these are the things which validate our authenticity? The attitudes and expectations rappers create through their words collectively can be more poisonous than the actual words of any particular rapper.

Studio Gangsters

In the early 90's, "gangster" rap (which will be defined in the next chapter) controlled the hip hop movement, making everybody gangsters or tough guys. To be noticed was a matter of being the gangster extreme. You either had to *be* a killer, be in the company of killers, or have been on some prison expedition in order to be recognized. During this time, the hip hop world coined the term "studio gangster." A studio gangster might put out a song about shooting, killing, carrying guns, or going to jail, but may have never done any of them. In other words, he was a gangster in the studio while doing an album but not really a gangster in the streets.

12

Since Hip Hop holds him accountable, that's just not acceptable. 50 Cent came out in 2003 with a song called "Wanksta," which became an updated version of the term "studio gangster." He was letting us know once again that, after 15 years, there were still imposters rapping about being killers who weren't real, excluding himself of course. In this song, 50 taunts fake gangster rappers, accusing them over and over again in his chorus of claiming to be gangsters even though they had never shot anyone. Again, the penalty for not being authentic means going before Hip Hop's Sanhedrin where you will be found guilty and sentenced to death as a hip hop artist. In his book *Queens Reigns Supreme: Fat Cat, 50 Cent and the Rise of the Hip Hop Hustler*, Ethan Brown addressed this merge of Hip Hop with hustlers.

> *"Hustlers became part of the ever-present hip-hop entourage or took on jobs as assistants, security guards, or managers. Hip-hop might have offered lower pay than hustling, but the risks associated with the streets were no longer worth the gamble. It was a mutually beneficial relationship. Hip-hoppers needed hustlers to bolster their street cred, especially with the ascent of gangster rap in the early nineties, which trumpeted values like realness and authenticity."*[2]

I am not suggesting that many of today's artists have never done crime or been in the streets, but the majority of them are simply trying to make a dollar with an image that *appeals* to the streets. The problem is that the act is landing entertainers and their audiences alike in graves or prisons.

Chapter Two

TUPAC SHAKUR, JESUS OF THE STREETS

H ip Hop began on the east coast in the boroughs of New York City. Inner city teens were galvanized by music that centered on energy, dancing, partying, and fun. This music was an escape from the harsh realities of ghetto life which offered little hope of deliverance. The music remained consistent with this theme even until the late 80's. In the early 90's, however, Hip Hop made a pilgrimage out west, and its message changed dramatically. In the west, inner city teens were dealing with a variety of struggles that had not been addressed in east coast rap. Hip Hop abandoned hypnotic beats and poetic lyrics for the more aggressive and explicit narratives that described the violent and harsh realities of different streets, giving birth to what was briefly mentioned in Chapter One as "gangster rap." One of the pioneers of this movement was a group called N.W.A. The acronym speaks for itself – it stands for "Niggas With Attitude." What came forth was music without remorse, regrets or repercussions. This music was harsh, even to the ears of Hip Hop's veterans who felt that their sacred art form was being vandalized by novices who were destroying, rather than protecting, this most precious craft. I can remember having heated discussions with my peers about how West Coast rappers couldn't rap. "Rap is about word play, not gun play," I would argue vehemently. Although there was controversy as to whether their rap remained true to hip hop roots, west coast rap artists did not feel the need to remain true to anything other than the streets. They were bent on making sure that the whole world understood what street life was really like regardless of who might be offended. Gangster rap exposed issues in the culture that smooth rhymes and lyrical flow just could not solve. Hip Hop was in need of a Savior – West Coast gangster rap made this clear and evident.

Hip Hop Screams Out

Hip Hop's move out west created what I call a "Blind Bartimaeus opportunity." In scripture (Mark 10:46-52), Blind Bartimaeus is described as a man who sits by the wayside while the multitudes follow Jesus. Scripture portrays him as a desperate man, frustrated by his deficiency, screaming out for Jesus. The crowds, seeking some miracle of their own, were completely cold and intolerant toward Bartimaeus and made attempts to silence him. Bartimaeus paid them no attention, and screaming all the louder, eventually captured Jesus' attention.

Before Jesus' arrival, I wonder how often Bartimaeus screamed out about his condition. I am pretty sure that his blindness saddened him from time to time, but it was probably something he had learned to live with. It was the way he was born; there wasn't much he could do about it; and that was his life. However, when Bartimaeus heard that Jesus was coming – the one who heals, raises the dead, and gives sight to the blind – suddenly, in him an expectation was created. As Jesus approached, the man screamed out as if he had *just been* struck blind! The possibility of his blindness being healed had just become a reality. He didn't know how to follow Jesus, couldn't find him, and had been living in darkness all of his life. He didn't know the "right" way to approach him, so he just screamed out, thinking, 'If I don't scream, he will never know my condition.'

Could Hip Hop be a sort of blind Bartimaeus, seeking a Savior the only way it knows how? Hip hop culture, in its hopeless condition, is screaming for Jesus from all angles. Now more than ever, we hear vulgar rap artists speak of God in interviews and in their music. "Jesus Walks" by rap mogul Kanye West (who will be discussed more in the next chapter) is Bartimaeus screaming at the top of his lungs for Jesus' attention. The discussion has less to do with whether West was right or wrong in making the song and more to do with the fact that using Jesus' name shows that he is attempting to connect to Him. It's a call for Jesus' attention. Hip Hop screams, and although philosophers, iconoclasts, atheists, radicals and even the nation of Islam have given their attention, Hip Hop is still screaming. Shamefully, the church, who has the real answer, hears this scream and goes into debate as to whether Hip Hop is theologically sound. Will we turn and give hip hop culture our undivided attention as Jesus did Bartimaeus? Too often, the church has been fused in with the crowd and has offered nothing but a cold stare of indifference. We become so fixated on the fact that *we* are walking with Jesus that Bartimaeus feels like a disturbance. Think about it: if the multitudes had brought him to Jesus themselves, he wouldn't have needed to scream out. Their indifference left him no other choice. Hip Hop says, 'My screams are vulgar to your ears because you interpret them that way, but what I'm actually saying is that it's my time – don't walk past me without attending to my needs.' The vulgarity of west coast rap embarrassed us as a society, much like the mother with a spoiled toddler who passes out in the middle of the grocery aisle because he can't have his way. She pretends that he should know better, but she knows that he doesn't. When we hear their scream, are we more focused on the *way* they scream out? Should we not focus on the cause of their scream? Deliverance isn't always as quiet as we would like it to be. The opening of blind Bartimaeus' uncivilized mouth ends up being the entrance for Jesus to get to his condition.

The Soft Side of the Gangster

After gangster rap scared all of America half to death, we were introduced to a different dimension of the gangster character. Between the crack sales, the gangbanging, and prison time, the thug suddenly developed a conscience. Of course, he still did his dirt, and his hustle continued. But every now and then, we began to catch him in those quiet moments pondering all he had done in life. Even those who respected his hardcore persona began to realize that he wasn't as cold or indifferent as he had portrayed himself. He *is* afraid at times. He does feel pain, emotions, and vulnerability. Through this particular style of hip hop music, the gangster became more approachable, and the general public could sympathize with this side of him, even admiring his plight through street obstacles. The group Geto Boys, whose lead rapper was Scarface, released a song called "My Mind is Playing Tricks on Me" that helped alter the way we viewed street hustlers. This song allowed the casual listener to replace judgment with compassion. The lyrics speak about a street hustler who had done a lifetime of dirt and was now struggling within himself to keep his sanity. He describes his life as being in a constant state of paranoia, expressing feelings of insecurity, fear, and guilt. Victimized by haunting nightmares that deprive him of sleep, he searches for an escape, even considering suicide. The usual bravado of the apathetic killer is relinquished; we seem, instead, to be diagnosing a schizophrenic who is trying to find the nearest exit as opposed to a hustler who has sold his soul to the game. This honest portrayal changed the mood of gangster rap. 'Yes, I'm out here on the corner, and I'm doing all that I am doing, but deep down inside, I hate what I've become.' Though it is hard to understand such complexities, these emotional contradictions are very real. I can remember the very first time I was the lead man in a robbery. That meant I would be the first man in – the voice demanding money from behind the pointed pistols. We had purposely chosen our target knowing that the staff would be all females. We wanted to encounter as few men as possible. We did not want any heroes! I can recall opening the door and screaming at the top of my lungs. This nearly scared the all-female staff half to death. To be honest I don't know if I was trying to scare them or scare all of the fear out of myself. As I watched the obviously traumatized woman bagging the money, I can recall feeling as if I was holding all of the women that I loved at gunpoint. She was shaking as she put the money in the bag, and I was probably more relieved when it was over than she was. We had gotten away, but I could never get away from myself and my own dreadful thoughts. The one thing I absolutely hated was being alone. Even before I was tried and convicted, the struggles that were going on inside of me were nearly unbearable and getting caught was, strangely enough, a relief. None of my peers knew of this struggle because they never saw me without a smile on my face. This is the essence of "My Mind is Playing Tricks on Me." One could be fooled by a gangster's tough persona, but this song helped break down the barriers that seemed impenetrable. Scarface helped father this style of rap, giving the thug a conscience and allowing it to be shared. He went out on a limb, sharing the secret emotions of the gangster. This, in turn, opened a floodgate of emotion from various street characters, rappers and entertainers.

The Gangster Finds His Voice in Tupac Shakur

If Scarface fathered this style, then his begotten son would have to be the late Tupac Shakur. He was the man who mastered the craft of emptying out the contents of his heart and making it a drinkable beverage, even for mainstream America. No one up to that point had gone to such lengths to articulate the mind, emotion and ambition of street individuals, at least not as an artist. Tupac was different. He brought clarity to the confusing behaviors of street youth, and with every opportunity, illuminated the complexities of the ghetto life. For example, when speaking of his difficult childhood growing up in the projects, he said,

> *"The same crime element that white people are scared of, black people are scared. The same crime element that white people fear, we fear. So we defend ourselves from the same crime element that they scared of, you know what I'm sayin'? So while they waiting for legislation to pass and everything, we next door to the killer. We next door to him cuz we in the projects with eighty niggaz in the building. All them killers they are letting out, they right there in that building. But it's better? Just cuz we black we get along with the killers or something? We get along with the rapists cause we black and we from the same hood? What is that? We need protection too."*[1]

Though his music was saturated with curse words and foul language, points such as these make you walk away from a song or an interview almost feeling guilty for holding a pointed finger. This was part of his mission – to add oil to the gangster rap "tin man," giving flexibility and creating new dimensions. The type of music he created moved the audience away from the tough exterior of the gangster and placed the focus on the internal issues of his heart and mind. As a result, we were convinced that there was a thug in all of us, from the slums to the upper echelon of the suburbs. He was speaking of struggles we could all relate to. Even real thugs liked Tupac because he told the true story that they had kept hidden from their homeboys and couldn't articulate themselves.

During the beginning of my incarceration, one thing that surprised me was how prevalent religion was within the confines of prison. It wasn't just Christianity; it was a little bit of everything. Everybody was looking to reach beyond himself toward something that transcended the brick walls and locked doors. What had previously been a symbol of power and significance, a nice car for some and nice apparel for others, was no longer accessible, thus forcing the human spirit to go deeper than material possessions to find leverage. The craziest thought in the world begins to come to your mind – 'Who am I?' This leads to the next crazy thought – 'Who is God?!!' As they were taking away my clothing and jewelry, replacing them with oversized orange jumpsuits, it amazed me that my entire worth could fit into a plastic bag and be placed in a drawer marked "Property." What frightened me most was the fact that I could actually disappear before my own eyes. I was housed with inmates from all over. I met kingpins who had charges in different countries and other guys who were accused of murder, rape, drugs and every other crime imaginable. The very first night they put me on the floor with other inmates, I remember seeing guys in the back corner of the hall gathering for a Bible study. I really didn't know what they were doing. I was trying my best to "mind my business." After the Bible study, they gathered in a circle for prayer and sang a few hymns. I was stunned. I had never thought that real thugs were on a quest to find God. At least, that's not the story that I had seen in magazines and videos. This picture didn't fit my definition of a gangster at all; to me, it seemed more like a compromise, a cop out. Many would be surprised to know how often hardcore thugs and gangsters, because of their brokenness, cry out to God in their own way. Living on the edge, whether in prison or not, puts you in such predicaments that, at some point, finding a power greater than your own is necessary. Because gangster rap dealt with gangbanging, shootouts, prison, and death, it's no surprise that Tupac embraced the concept of god. It is in the darkest moments of people's lives that they cry out to God, and gangster rap reflects Hip Hop's darkest hours. This is what Tupac was trying to tell us in his music.

Tupac Intercedes on Behalf of the Streets

If I had to pick a song which clearly illustrates Tupac's place in life as it pertained to God, it would have to be the song "Shed So Many Tears." In this song, he pours himself out to God, explaining the depravity of his life. Attempting to offer a guilty plea, Tupac begs God to accept him and restore him to right standing. He makes himself vulnerable to God while still managing to maintain his gangster persona. This song is a sad depiction of a young man who seems hopeless. What is paramount is to note that Tupac is actually addressing God directly. The spiritual connotation of his messages made his music a revival, and the streets gathered around by the masses. Tupac initiated contact and created dialogue with God in a way no one else in Hip Hop had done before. With the boldness of a true gangster, he approached, and even questioned, a God we as a hip hop audience were more or less afraid of. Tupac would probably not get credit for this, but he helped the culture become cognizant that there was a God. Before him, Hip Hop had been dominated by New York style rap, which was embedded in a belief system called the Five Percent Nation. This doctrine is established in the belief that the black man himself is God. This belief has always been prevalent in prison and in Hip Hop. Five Percent belief focuses on self-sufficiency, knowledge of self, and self-empowerment. Five Percenters even refer to each other as God. In the mid and late nineties, artists such as Wu-Tang Clan, Nas, and Busta Rhymes, led the way in attempting to completely remove the power and influence of God from rap music. Nowadays, however, just about every major rapper includes a song about God. This is largely because Tupac acknowledged that there was indeed a power beyond man.

Tupac's music wrote Hip Hop in as the prodigal child – the son who is in the pigpen eating slop and has seemingly forgotten his royal inheritance. Out of the blue, he remembers that he has a father. He hasn't gotten up yet; he is still stuck in the mire of the pen; and you can't even tell the great thing that has taken place because, physically, he's in the same location. However, inside his mind, something groundbreaking has occurred – he begins to admit his need for a father. This is what Tupac's music did. It allowed Hip Hop to acknowledge its need for God. After Tupac, it didn't seem so strange or offensive to mention God, and it also became more acceptable to imbue Hip Hop with spiritual issues.

The Righteous Thug

What was truly detrimental, however, is that Tupac could never show us how to properly develop a relationship with God. Instead, he remained in the pigpen, looking towards the mansion and only remembering the Father. We, as his audience, have stayed there, too.

Instead of getting up out of the slop, Tupac actually made an attempt to bring God into the pigpen with him. Refusing to change his lifestyle, Tupac broadened the road that was once narrow and seemingly changed what God would accept. Tupac made all attempts during his rap career to persuade God to come out of heaven and hang out in the hood. Those in the streets were sure that he had accomplished this task. Thugs reached out to God but remained rooted in street principles. The sanctification process never happened. The weed remained in Hip Hop's pocket, the alcohol on his breath, and the girls on his lap. He set his own rules. This vantage point became Hip Hop's newly found religion – keeping the familiar lifestyle yet gaining a relationship with God. Michael Dyson, in his book *Holler If You Hear Me*, called it "thug theology." He writes,

> *"The readiness to die is characteristic of thug theology, as much because of the intensity of the suffering they observe and endure...as the belief that they have squared themselves with God."* [2]

Tupac and his followers became the equivalent of the Danites in the Old Testament, not just having a lukewarm relationship with God, but profanely incorporating God into their evil ways and actions.

Tupac the High Priest

Judges 18 tells us the story of the Danites who were the smallest of the tribes of Israel and, therefore, the last to receive their land. They had difficulty fighting to take the land that God had allotted to them, so they sought out easier means. They became renegades, looting and taking by their own will instead of receiving their blessing from God. In the midst of their travels, they came upon the house of a man named Micah. Judges 17 tells how Micah had hired his own, illegitimate priest. The

24

Danites questioned this priest for guidance, asking him if they would have success in attacking and burning down the surrounding cities, and he told them that they would. The priest proved to be correct, so they returned and stole him away from Micah. Why would they steal an illegitimate priest? The Danites stole the priest because he represented a connection, a link, a bridge back to God. The priest was Israel's mediator and intercessor; everybody had to go through a priest to be made right with God. The Danites found themselves outside of God's people and outside of God's will. In their minds, taking another man's priest and having success meant that God was with them. They now felt that they could take God wherever they wanted to go and be justified in doing so.

The Danites found an alternate route; they literally stole a high priest, and strong-armed themselves into a position of righteousness, so it seemed. This was their way of finding God, but in doing away with the consistent standards and accountability of the people who had a relationship with God, the Danites were symbolically barging into God's favor and doing away with the method that God Himself had set in place.

Tupac's music and the movement it created became an alternate route for the streets in a similar way. Tupac was Hip Hop's stolen high priest – the go-between, the man in the middle, the intercessor offering up prayers and sacrifices. In his music, he went before God explaining the difficult circumstances of growing up in poverty-stricken neighborhoods and prisons – mothers on drugs, families in gangs, and friends in graves. Tupac spoke as a defense attorney, copping a plea with God. He did so not only for himself but also for the streets, hoping that God would, in turn, justify street life. The church said that God had a case against the evils of Hip Hop; Tupac turned and said "Only God Can Judge Me" (the title of one of his songs) in challenge. This significantly changed the

25

demeanor of Hip Hop. Instead of humbly developing a relationship with the church, he was now arrogantly saying, 'I no longer need you; I can get to God by myself.' In his song "Blasphemy," Tupac attempts to dismantle church authority and doctrine. He begins by accusing the preacher of being a liar and using the pulpit to gain riches. He also suggests that the preacher is demonizing our children, placing unwarranted guilt on them. Challenging the church's doctrine of hell, Tupac claims to witness hell on earth every day when he sees the struggles of a crack addict. Finally, he pushes the preacher aside, disregarding church authority, and interprets Jesus' compassionate side by saying that Jesus understands the crimes that are committed by gangsters or thugs. All of these challenges to Christianity occur in a few lines which last only seconds in the song but become a consistent theme of Tupac's music and message. Just as the Danites did, the streets turned their backs on God's established order, picked up idols, and ran with a sure winner. Tupac, his music and his movement, gave the "yes" that was needed to continue the mission in the streets.

Tupac, the Christ

Jesus told his disciples, "Watch out that no one deceives you. For many will come in my name, claiming, 'I am the Christ,' and will deceive many." (Matthew 24:4-5) He also said, "For false Christs and false prophets will appear and perform great signs and miracles to deceive even the elect—if that were possible." (Matthew 24:24) Notice the scripture says that there shall arise "Christs." I argue that Tupac is to be mentioned as one. Everybody, from the intellectuals to those in the streets, will follow or be tempted to follow a Christ of some sort; there will be false Christs on different levels and for different walks of life. Tupac packaged

26

salvation in a way that was readily accessible to the streets. He was Hip Hop's supposed savior. Tupac gave the streets an alternate route to salvation, which gave the false pretense that the thug lifestyle had been accepted by God. Tupac's lyrics were by design; the spiritual undertones were intentional. His music was ordered, disciplined, and repetitious. We learned his mind and methods quickly and practiced them in the streets. We became Tupac's disciples, quoting his lines as much as the Bible-savvy quote Proverbs. His music was our gospel; thug life was our religion; Tupac became our Christ. Of course, he's usually recognized only for his gangster rap stigma, but his spiritual influence goes much deeper than the average listener would ever fathom. Tupac didn't specifically say that he was the Christ, but he became a Christ-type to his followers.

Thug Life, the Religion

Thug Life, the phrase Tupac had emblazoned across his abdomen, was not just another tattoo he got on a whim or a dare. It represented a culture in and of itself – one for which he lived to establish and died to maintain. For Tupac, THUG LIFE was an acronym pointed at white America. It stood for "The Hate U Gave Little Infants F---s Everybody." Tupac's life exemplified the struggle that comes from being a byproduct of America's ghetto, welfare system, and substandard public school system – the project that emerged from the projects. With his tenacious lyrics and lifestyle, he became a caricature of the inner city youth with no hope and nowhere to turn. Keeping his gangster persona even as he advanced in life was his way of getting back at America. His message was: 'Imagine how many young black minds are demented, self destructive and think like me because of you. I'm the gangster you created, America, but don't want to deal with. America, I am your child.

27

You raised me to be this way.' Tupac was hoping that his erratic, outlandish behavior would prove that the black child is being neglected by America's social system.

Another dimension of this movement aside from social activism was Thug Life, the institution. Tupac was actually attempting to establish an infrastructure which would be governed by gang leaders and street hustlers. It would include a code of ethics that would serve as street laws and regulations to which they would all adhere. The purpose was that thugs, hustlers, and gangsters would take on the responsibility of making their own streets safer instead of depending on the government that continued to fail in its attempts. It almost seemed as if Tupac was establishing Thug Life as something positive for the community. The question, however, is what the streets understood Thug Life to mean. Regardless of what an artist says concerning his music, what is significant, especially in Hip Hop, is the lifestyle the artist exhibits. Inevitably, what he says is going to be interpreted through the filter of what we see him doing. We didn't understand that Tupac was trying to bring the hood together on a positive accord; neither did we know that his mission was a mission of peace. Tupac intended Thug Life to be a movement for unity and empowerment for the streets. However, because his lifestyle was so inconsistent with this message, the part of it that remained intact was hate towards the white America power structure. Thug Life was to be a belief system, a code by which we could live. Unfortunately for Tupac, most of us did not know or even understand what the acronym T-h-u-g L-i-f-e stood for. We understood society's idea of a thug, and, inspired by Tupac's living example, we did our very best to convey that image. What was even more impressionable is that we were able to see Tupac personify our image of Thug Life right before our eyes. It was fresh, alive, and invigorating because he was learning and teaching it at the same time. Until he became a successful artist, Tupac had not been charged with any crime. He even admitted that he had tried to hustle earlier in life but failed miserably. There he was, caught between representing a voice of the culture through study, much like a journalist, and getting too close to the culture, thereby becoming a great exaggeration of even the worst character it has to offer. Was it Tupac who created Thug Life or did Thug Life create Tupac? We witnessed with him as he was vindicated of allegedly shooting the police and waited with him as he did prison time for an alleged rape. We watched reports of him getting shot five times and making it through. We saw him and his entourage stomping a man on camera, and finally, we saw him shot and killed. Thug Life pushed him to a standard of living that was impossible to maintain without dying or going to jail. In fact, Thug life pushed all of its participants to the point of life and death everyday at every moment. This was one of the reasons our youth were drawn to it – for the risk factor. Even Tupac himself was not dismissed from this. Thug life made gangsters, hustlers, soldiers, and even martyrs. This was its meaning, and this was the call.

"Ride or die" – this was the challenge that initiated many to thug life's call. It's a question Tupac coined and used repeatedly in his music. In laymen's terms, the question "ride or die" is asking: 'Are you with me until death do us part – whatever the mission, whatever the task?' It was the streets' marriage vow, promising one's life to a cause. It's a question asked from one to another that ensures commitment to the highest degree. It is usually used when there's a serious situation at hand. "Ride or die" is what separated the followers from the true believers, the talkers from the doers, the spectators from the "riders." Scripture tells us, "From this time many of his disciples turned back and no longer followed him."

29

(John 6:66) Jesus had just given his followers a hard word of doctrine. He asks his disciples, "'You do not want to leave too, do you?'... Simon Peter answered him, 'Lord to whom shall we go? You have the words of eternal life.'" (John 6:67-68) This was a "ride or die" situation which promoted the true disciples from the rest. Tupac, moving in the likeness of Christ, wanted the assurance that partakers of Thug Life were disciples who pledged their allegiance and their life. What Tupac was doing went further than just turning friends into soldiers. His music became an instruction manual for survival in the streets. Tupac set the standards of accountability and conduct. In the song "Bomb First," he actually asks how many of his followers would be willing to die for him. This is not just a rhetorical question. It is real and true to the Thug Life law and code of ethics.

Tupac, the Prophet

Jesus' own words and earthly assignment propelled him towards capital punishment, death on the cross. He prophesied of his death and taught that it was to be his ultimate sacrifice. Jesus even brought glory to the cross in his teachings, challenging his disciples by saying, "...anyone who does not take his cross and follow me is not worthy of me." (Matthew 10:38) Tupac did this as well. He is often quoted as having said, "All good niggers, all the niggers who change the world, die in violence. They don't die in regular ways."[3] Tupac had the understanding that he would die in violence and even categorized himself as a man who was significant enough to change the world. Tupac always prepared his followers, as Jesus did his disciples, for the day he would be leaving, never allowing us as the listening audience to put any trust in the idea of growing old with him. In the song "If I Die 2Nite," he speaks of future headlines that would tell of his murder and asks his followers not to weep for him. Tupac actually specifies that his death would come by way of murder. In a poem he wrote entitled "In the Event of My Demise," he says,

> *"In the event of my demise*
> *When my heart can beat no more*
> *I hope I die for a principle*
> *Or a belief that I had lived 4*
> *I will die before my time*
> *Because I feel the shadow's depth*
> *So much I wanted 2 accomplish*
> *Before I reached my death*
> *I have come 2 grips with the possibility*
> *And wiped the last tear from my eyes*
> *I loved all who were positive*
> *In the event of my demise."* [4]

Not only did he rap and write about his death, he also played it out in the music video for the song "I Ain't Mad At Cha." In the video, he was gunned down while walking out the door with a friend. The paramedics were unable to keep him from dying. This is similar to how he actually died. In 1996, while leaving a boxing match in Las Vegas, Tupac and the owner of Death Row Records, Suge Knight, were riding in a car as an unidentified assailant pulled up and began shooting into the car. Tupac was hit. He died in the hospital six days later from respiratory failure and cardiac arrest. Scripture says that "...false Christs and false prophets will appear and perform great signs and miracles to deceive even the elect – if that were possible." (Matthew 24:24) It cannot be denied that Tupac indeed envisioned his death, solidifying himself as a prophet to his disciples.

Tupac, the Sacrifice

Jesus said, "...I lay down my life – only to take it up again. No one takes it from me, but I lay it down of my own accord. I have authority to lay it down and authority to take it up again..." (John 10:17-18) In reference to his betrayal, Jesus told Judas to go and do it quickly. He then went with the other disciples to a place where Judas knew he would be. This places Judas' strategy within Jesus' greater strategy. Judas' betrayal and his death did not take Jesus by surprise. He knew it was going to happen and even played a part in deciding when it would happen. In the book entitled "Tupac: Resurrection 1971–1996," Tupac is quoted as saying,

> *"Now I got every man in America who wants to take an order from me, you know what I'm sayin, who wants to know what I want to do, or what's my plan for young black males. And that makes me scared. But that makes me want to rise to the occasion. Makes me wanna give my whole life to 'em, and I will give my whole life to this plan I have for thug life."[5]*

Tupac consciously gave his life as a sacrifice for thug life. In doing so, he changes his imminent death from a murder to a willing sacrifice. Therefore, he dies seemingly by design, taking the sting out of death and turning it into an opportunity to advance his cause. In his song "Death Around the Corner," he claims that real gangsters will not only die but will approach death without fear and choose when it happens. Tupac seemingly picks his time, becoming the ultimate sacrifice for what he believed in. Just as Jesus did, Tupac led by example, and as a result, many of his followers have blindly sacrificed their lives for the cause.

Thug Life, the Spirit

Jesus promised his disciples that, after he passed, they would do greater exploits and would be operating out of the power of the Holy Spirit. In John 14, Jesus said that he had to leave in order to make room for the Spirit. Similarly, Tupac's death solidified and activated the thug life movement, propelling it to a level beyond even his own capabilities. Tupac the man was one thing, but the spirit of thug life has become far more dangerous. In his song "Outlaw," Tupac makes the claim that he will never die but instead multiply through thug life disciples. He knew that he was leaving behind a legacy that the entire world would fear and respect – a generation of youth who worshipped his words and would promise to carry out the mission. As is true of any other icon, Tupac has become bigger in death than he was in life. He's no longer bound by a place or a location; he is on t-shirts, in magazines, MTV, BET; he is in the people, and he is everywhere. Tupac would spend days recording while he was living, knowing his time was short. Even now, ten years after his death, some of his music is still being released. This keeps his doctrine fresh in the minds of today's youth and also creates the "feel" that he is still with us. Tupac is raising yet another generation. Some even refer to him in the present tense, much like Christians refer to Christ.

Tupac's spirit also lives on through the music and message of many of today's prominent hip hop superstars. Everyone – 50 Cent, Eminem, DMX, The Game, T.I. – gives him homage as their king, often even quoting him directly in their music. They carry on the spirit of thug life, mixing spirituality with gangster ambitions and justifying the heinous activities of street life. They perpetuate the idea that the streets can be in right standing with God, changing what God accepts instead of changing themselves. This spirit continues to have a major impact on the direction and focus of hip hop culture today.

Tupac Preparing a Mansion

Is there a place in heaven for a gangster? Tupac often asked this question in his music. He even dedicated a song to the idea called "I Wonder if Heaven Got a Ghetto." The question solidified his music as a spiritual movement. Completing his mission as the street's messiah, he ushered street culture to its triumphant destination, a final place of rest. In asking this question, Tupac is actually implying that God understands and excuses the explicit and outlandish behavior of the streets. He suggests that God has a place for thug life and has given the outlaw angel wings.

In an exclusive interview with *VIBEonline*, Tupac answers questions about religion saying,

> *"So I believe God blesses us, I believe God blesses those that hustle. Those that use their minds and those that overall are righteous. I believe that everything you do bad comes back to you. So everything that I do that's bad, I'm going to suffer for it. But in my heart, I believe what I'm doing in my heart is right. So I feel like I'm going to heaven."* [6]

In Tupac's song "Thugz Mansion," he opens by speaking to those that are tired of gangbanging and getting arrested by the police. He imagines a gangster's paradise – a place they can all coexist in peace. He ends the song petitioning God to reserve for him a place in heaven. Tupac is actually suggesting that there is a mansion in Heaven designated for the gangster. Remember, Jesus said, "In My Father's house are many mansions; if it were not so, I would have told you. I go to prepare a place for you." (John 14:2) According to Tupac, if the streets would give their life over to his plan of salvation, he promises a place and a God who would receive all of their pain and troubles. One would not have to change his lifestyle. He would only need to follow the ways of Tupac to a heavenly abode where God the Father awaits.

Conclusion

We have now established Tupac as a Christ-type – a priest interceding for the streets, a prophet predicting his death, a sacrificial lamb for the culture, and a king revered by his peers. We've also seen how he established thug life, the religion that offers a heaven for the gangster and lives on as a spirit driving the culture. It is clear that Tupac had an agenda in mind. His purpose was not just to entertain but to create a faith, belief and trust in a god who had formerly seemed aloof. As a kind of ambassador, he indoctrinated a generation, making God and heaven tangible. As we look to evangelize hip hop culture, we have to go with this understanding – Hip Hop's disciples don't see that they need you, your Bibles, or your God. Tupac has already given them a belief system that, to them, is sufficient. They are not seeking for something else. Our mission, therefore, is to dismantle this false doctrine and establish their need for true salvation.

I placed this chapter discussing Tupac early in the book so that there would be no doubt about my response to hip hop culture. Clearly, this culture has received a complete word and doctrine that neither lines up with God's word nor is seeking the church's approval. Understanding the evils of Hip Hop does not absolve us of our responsibilities to deal with and relate to those who are in the culture. It gives us all the more reason to establish a voice in their world. There are so many that have never known any other truth. In the next chapters, I will develop a perspective and strategy that I believe is essential to evangelizing hip hop culture. As you read about the artists and their lyrics, don't be distracted by how offensive they may seem to your Christian ears. I've already established that this culture is in need of a savior. As a church body, we must be objective and develop a balanced approach, deriving a strategy from the wisdom of God's word.

Chapter Three

KANYE WEST: SHOULD "JESUS WALK" IN OUR CHURCH?

Early one morning after I had finished jogging, I began fishing through some of the local radio stations. I'm always spying out hip hop culture; I consider it my Canaan land. I came across a song and was enraptured by what seemed to be a revolutionary war chant. Before I could even gather myself, I was carried away, bobbing my head to the beat. I usually investigate a song's lyrics before giving my stamp of approval, but this time it was too late. I was taken under, drowning helplessly, gasping for air as I heard the lyrics making the claim that Jesus walks with hustlers, killers, murderers, and even strippers! What?!! Jesus!?? This is a track about Jesus!?? I couldn't believe it. I checked again just to make sure I was in the right place, and I was; it was playing on one of my town's high-energy hip hop stations. Immediately, I turned it up louder, wailing and pumping my fist in the air, hoping I wouldn't discover any subtle disagreement. I called my partner Shane, ecstatic about my findings, as if I had discovered a treasure chest.

"This is the one we've been looking for! This is our open window to the culture! The hip hop heads are going to go wild about this one!"

Then, right in the middle of my celebration, I was humbled by this thought -- church folk will not like this one. "Murderers, niggas, strippers" (various words mentioned in the song) – what is that? Lord, how would I explain? How could I open their eyes to see the potential for ministry in this song? In my mind I began to perfect my argument. This song establishes that Jesus is not some mythical figure nailed to a cross, and coming from a cultural icon such as Kanye West, this is groundbreaking. He isn't just using the name in passing; it is actually the title of the song, "Jesus Walks!" It's a hook that our youth will grasp easily and mimic. Yo! Jesus the Christ has stepped out of heaven to walk with us! He's alive, he's alive says Kanye West!

Still yet, I pictured myself standing in front of the church getting hit in the head with yet another rock, thrown from the direction of the deacon board. In this chapter, I'm hoping to convince them to put down their rocks. Before we go any further, please understand that I am not asking the church to go out and buy the latest Kanye West CD. What I do believe is that he represents a move within hip hop culture that is looking our way, and we should take advantage of it.

Hip Hop Transitions From "God" to Jesus

As discussed previously, Tupac was Hip Hop in the pigpen at the point of acknowledging the father. If this is the case, then Kanye West would be Hip Hop getting up and heading towards home. West specifically said "Jesus," not just God. I do not know if Kanye West is a Christian or not, but what he represents is a culture that finally has its eyes pointed toward the direction of the church. Hip Hop, as a sojourner, has moved from coast to coast and every place in between. The song "Jesus Walks" propels Hip Hop towards a place that offers true deliverance. Jesus, the name, represents home, a final destination of rest and refuge. Hip Hop, this seemingly fatherless child, refuses the temporary shelter of the pigpen and screams out "Jesus" as if he is family, as if he belongs. We only know of him taking his inheritance and spending his money on riotous living (strip clubs, weed, alcohol, etc.) The church looks at him in sharp rebuttal and says, 'Where do you think you're going? How dare you call on the name of our Father?' Hip Hop responds, 'I know my body still reeks of the pigpen, and I have all the residue of bad decisions clinging to me. I am filthy. I am absolutely detestable. My pants are hanging, and I'm sportin' a doo rag with blood shot eyes and pain that runs deep. But I'm singing my heart out that Jesus walks. I haven't gotten there yet, but I'm on my way. Jesus Walks!' Of course, this seems hypocritical and sends a mixed message, but that's because we're catching him between the pigpen and the mansion. That is exactly where the culture is; this theme echoes throughout their music. Although this idea does not sit well with most people, it takes a deeper look to see what's taking place in the heart of Hip Hop. We want to either confirm that he belongs to the Father or push him back in the direction from which he came. The problem is that Hip Hop is a traveler and hasn't called any place home. Now that traveler is looking in our direction. It would make it so much easier to ignore him if he just wasn't screaming "Jesus walks" in our ears.

No Ordinary Name

JESUS. What other name creates such effortless confrontation? Whether it is Jesus walking, Jesus jumping, or Jesus dancing, many hate the name even being mentioned. Jesus said, "...I did not come to bring peace but a sword... a man's enemies will be members of his own household." (Matthew 10:34,36) In other words, my name and who I am will cause a great rift that divides people and provokes controversy. Due to Hip Hop's aggressive, war-like nature, it's not surprising to me that God would use it as a tool to pick a fight with the conscience of America. In a line from the song "Jesus Walks," Kanye West boldly confronts the music industry, claiming that he could rap about absolutely anything, even sex, but if he speaks of Jesus, his record will not be played. He challenges even his own colleagues, daring them to play music that agitates the conventional mindset.

Ever since the birth of the early church, the name Jesus and persecution have gone hand in hand. Peter, John, and the apostles were beaten severely for using Jesus' name. Concerning them, the Sanhedrin said,

> " *What are we going to do with these men?...Everybody living in Jerusalem knows they have done an outstanding miracle, and we cannot deny it. But to stop this thing from spreading any further among the people, we must warn these men to speak no longer to anyone in this name.* " (Acts 4:16-17)

In other words, the disciples could heal the sick, preach the gospel, and give sight to the blind, but not in the name of Jesus. Although the disciples did not waver under this threat, modern day believers struggle with this. There may not be an actual beating or imprisonment, but we are still intimidated when we're not in Christian surroundings. You hear it all the time from athletes, artists, and even some Christian artists – 'I would like to thank *God* for this great accomplishment.' These same people may profess Jesus Christ as their Lord and Savior, but are hushed by the muzzle of compromise when they know that using His name may

40

offend their audience. Jesus will not be silenced, even if it means using the big ego and big mouth of Hip Hop to be heard.

Confession Leads to Salvation

In October of 2002, Kanye West was in an almost fatal car accident; he had fallen asleep behind the wheel of his car. In the "Jesus Walks" remix, which was also played on the radio, he dedicated a verse to this crash giving God credit for saving his life. The story itself is moving, but West went beyond the simply tear-jerking inspiration and pronounced "Jesus walks!" He could have resorted to the ever-so-popular clichés: "Angels were watching over me," "The Man Upstairs," or "The Powers that be;" – we've heard them all. But after the smoke cleared, Jesus Christ was being preached on stages, in interviews, and anywhere else West could give his testimony. Even if you are not a rap fan, or like my mom, you just cannot understand the lyrics, his message is clear. Jesus is real and a present help in the time of need. Whoever would have thought that the rhymes and rhythms of hip hop music would lead us to the gospel of Jesus Christ? Let me explain why Kanye saying this is so important for the mission to save hip hop culture.

Regardless of whether T.D. Jakes is preaching or Kanye West is spitting a verse on the mic, the name Jesus will *always* be synonymous with salvation. After having been abducted, Peter addressed the Sanhedrin saying, "Salvation is found in no one else, for there is no other name under heaven given to men by which we must be saved." (Acts 4:12) Also scripture says, "That if you confess with your mouth, 'Jesus is Lord,' and believe in your heart that God raised him from the dead, you will be saved." (Romans 10:9) If confession of Jesus walking is in the mouth of this hip hop generation, could this not be the first step in the process of salvation? We are so accustomed to seeing people coming to the altar and confessing that Jesus is their Lord and Savior. This takes only moments and we say that they have received salvation. However, we can't necessarily see the process of them "believing" with their hearts. We just trust that that step has taken place. To some, "Jesus Walks" will just be a song with a hot beat, but for others, it just might be the catalyst for their salvation. This confession by Kanye West (a representative of hip hop culture) may have begun with his mouth, but it may soon end up in his heart.

In John 9, Jesus healed a man who had been blind since birth. This man, unlike blind Bartimaeus, was not screaming for Jesus' attention. Instead, Jesus was the initiator and decided to use this man's ailment for God's glory. He spat on the ground to make clay, placed it on the man's eyes, and told him to go wash in the pool. Since Jesus did not go with him, the blind man did not have the opportunity to see his healer. After he was healed, those that had always known the man to be blind couldn't believe that he could now see. They asked him how his eyes were opened, and he responded by saying, "The man they call Jesus made some mud and put it on my eyes..." (John 9:11) Remember, he does not know Jesus or even what He looks like. So, the men go to the Pharisees looking for some spiritual insight that would validate this miracle. Of course, the Pharisees ask the man the same thing, and he gives them the same response. The Pharisees, baffled by his healing and confession, call in the parents of the man for questioning. His parents confirm that he was born blind but put the responsibility on their son to tell his own story because they were afraid. The man continued to confess that it was Jesus who had healed him, so the Pharisees cast him out of the temple. Scripture tells us,

"Jesus heard that they had thrown him out, and when he found him, he said, 'Do you believe in the Son of Man?' 'Who is he, sir?' the man asked. 'Tell me so that I may believe in him.' Jesus said, 'You have now seen him; in fact, he is the one speaking with you.' Then the man said, 'Lord, I believe,' and he worshiped him." (John 9:35-38)

Initially in dealing with this man, Jesus healed him and then walked away. The man was left with a story about Jesus but didn't even know who He was. Eventually, Jesus made his way back to the man so that he could believe (not just confess) in Him and receive salvation. The man was not saved because of his confession that Jesus had healed him, but his confession made it possible for him to have a second encounter with Jesus, which led to his salvation and belief in his heart. "Jesus Walks" is an example of how hip hop is beginning to confess the reality of Jesus in this world. Since confession is the first step to salvation, we can only believe that God is ultimately leading this culture to a second encounter -- the one that will lead to souls being saved.

King of the Hill

Since the beginning of hip hop music, artists have devoted their entire careers to being crowned lords and gods - superheroes of unrealistic proportions. Right now, Kanye West is king of the mountain. He is the commander and chief of an army that's taking over as Hip Hop changes the dynamics of youth in America. Hip Hop is insinuating itself into every dimension of American culture. Nelly and country artist Tim Mcgraw collaborated on a hit single; Cadillac offered a Snoop Deville; Reebok merged with 50 Cent and Jay-Z is doing video commercials while Monday night football is on the air. Even colleges are offering classes studying Tupac's life. Our rap stars are becoming movie stars, and our athletes are becoming, well, *impersonating*, rappers. Everybody from Allen Iverson, Kobe Bryant, and Shaquille O'Neil has attempted to do their own hip hop album. Cementing his iconic status, Kanye West was even featured on the cover of the August 2005 edition of *Time* magazine. He's one of the most sought after characters in the game, and as of now, everything he touches is going platinum. He's respected as a rapper, but because of his superior producing abilities, he's also highly esteemed in other genres of music. Hip hop culture continuously escapes the boundaries of rap and expands its borders. The world is submitting to the reign of hip hop culture.

No kingdom has ever been established outside of God's sovereignty, and Hip Hop is no exception. God is still on the throne, and He's dealing with hip hop kings in a way that is familiar to how he dealt with Old Testament rulers.

> *"...the Lord moved the heart of Cyrus king of Persia to make a proclamation throughout his realm and to put it in writing: 'This is what Cyrus king of Persia says: 'The LORD, the God of heaven, has given me all the kingdoms of the earth and he has appointed me to build a temple for him at Jerusalem in Judah.'"* (Ezra 1:1-2)

King Cyrus, a gentile king who had the entire world under his control, looked up and acknowledged God. He wasn't referring to a god in general, but *the* God, maker of heaven and earth, the God of the children of Israel. Most importantly, he was moved by God to restore the city of Jerusalem. This is the same city and people that had been enslaved under his dominion. What boggles the mind is that scripture doesn't tell us that King Cyrus was suddenly converted, or that he began following the laws and rituals of the children of Israel. Neither does scripture say that he made his own people adhere to this strange god. He remained King Cyrus in nature and power, but God began the building process of Jerusalem through him. This is also seen in the case of King Solomon. Every nation around him wanted to have connection and covenant with him because of the glory and power that he represented. They gave gifts unto him to be on his side. Did all of these nations convert and turn to his God? No, but their resources helped build God's kingdom.

The Heart of the King is in the Hand of the Lord

Now, if our God could place a passion in the heart of King Cyrus to build a house for His people, why couldn't He charge Kanye West to do the same? Kanye West is an icon, a king of sorts. Is it so far-fetched to believe that God, wanting to rebuild and mend the lives of those under the guise of hip hop culture, would start by using someone who has actually played a part in making the people of this culture his subjects? Why *not* use Kanye West?

As our young people are bullied by "foreign kings" and their idols, Christian principles continue to lie in utter ruins. Look at our young men and women and tell me who their king is. Who do they adhere to? What voice do they receive in our public schools? The invading armies have burned down just about all traces of what was left of Godly living. MTV is the DJ for American culture, as we dance before the gods of weed, sex, money, and many other false idols. Then, all of a sudden, Kanye West proclaims "Jesus Walks," clearing off land for Christians in his place of rulership. Of course, this may seem suspicious coming from a king that doesn't have any special stock in God's people, but it is scriptural. "The king's heart is in the hand of the Lord; he directs it like a watercourse wherever he pleases." (Proverbs 21:1) The song "Jesus

Walks" is a perfect display of God's omnipotent hand still yet in total control.

The question many Christians then ask is: If you are going to promote Kanye West's music, what happens when young people see him endorsing and participating in all of Hip Hop's many vices? In response, let's take a closer look at the children of Israel rebuilding the temple. As they were building on foreign soil, the nations that surrounded them said that they wanted to assist in their building.

> *"When the enemies of Judah and Benjamin heard that the exiles were building a temple for the Lord, the God of Israel, they came to Zerubbabel and to the heads of the families and said, 'Let us help you build because, like you, we seek your God and have been sacrificing to him since the time of Esarhaddon king of Assyria, who brought us here.' But Zerubbabel, Jeshua and the rest of the heads of the families of Israel answered, 'You have no part with us in building a temple to our God. We alone will build it for the LORD, the God of Israel...'"*

(Ezra 4:1-3)

The only thing that we need is a "yes" from the king to start building. After a song like "Jesus Walks," many wanted to make Kanye West a saint and tell him that he is now responsible to live according to Christian principles. However, he is simply giving us an opportunity to build a Christian city inside his hip hop world. He gives me the chance to establish the city upon the hill, the one that will affect and win over his hip hop nation. We are building this city to challenge those who are under his influence. This does not mean that we will allow him to participate in building character, morality, or integrity in the young people who are under our influence. Once he tells me that I can build, I will take over from there. I am not handing him a hammer, a nail, a screwdriver, a shovel… nothing! Therefore, I am not disappointed when Kanye West does not measure up to Christian standards. He is simply a "yes," a doorway into his kingdom. Until his confession comes to fruition, I will view Kanye West as a type of King Cyrus, and we should teach our children to do the same as well.

Favor From the King is But for a Season

We have many examples of King Cyrus in our everyday lives. He is the boss or supervisor that talks about church whenever you come around. No, he may not be a Christian, but he respects your convictions, making sure not to do anything to offend your beliefs. He recognizes you as a good worker and shows you favor. Why? He feels that to violate you is to violate God, so he tries to stay on your good side. He may be a totally different person when you are not around. He is nasty, makes rude gestures and tells explicit jokes. Those who truly know him know a completely different nature. The point is that you don't expect him to be consistent in his actions, but you still operate in the favor that he gives. If we learn to see Kanye West in this manner, we will not be surprised when his next video displays half-naked girls. If we teach our young people these ideas, they will be able to view him as a King Cyrus of the hip hop nation. They will understand that, although he speaks of Jesus, he is not to be viewed as the next poster child for hip hop Christianity.

We are simply using his favor in this season, as long as it lasts. We will build as much as we can, as fast as we can, because his favor may not always be there. Outside influences can change a king's heart when he's not rooted in a relationship with God. Although he allowed the rebuilding of the temple at the beginning of his reign, King Artaxerxes later suspended the work because of advice he received from those who opposed the Israelites. King Herod had John the Baptist imprisoned, but didn't kill him until after he made a promise to his daughter-in-law. A *dance* put the head of John the Baptist on a platter. Although King Nebuchadnezzar highly favored Daniel, he had him thrown in the lion's den, again because of the trickery of those who wished to advance their own agendas. A king's "yes" can quickly turn into a king's "no." Next year, Kanye West may turn and blaspheme Jesus, so while he's still performing "Jesus Walks," I will use it to save as many souls who are under his influence as possible. We pray that Kanye West comes to the point of completely living for Jesus, but until then, we must use these examples from the word of God to show our young people that this fickle behavior does exist.

"Jesus Walks" Upsets the Church

So why are we so offended? Maybe it's because we don't think that Kanye West has the right or privilege to say such things about a God whom we don't perceive he is serving wholeheartedly. How dare he say "nigga" and the "s" word with such ease in the same song that speaks of Jesus walking! This type of confession should be coming from a Christian artist who loves the Lord fervently. My stance on this issue, which will later be explained in more detail, is probably not the most popular among my Christian peers; however, I am sure that we can all agree that the entire world needs to hear about Christ. Jesus called us to be evangelists, taking the gospel into places where it has never been heard. Though I love Christian rap artists such as Cross Movement and Da T.R.U.T.H., and they have several songs on their CD's which are just as profound, they are not nearly as respected by the world's standard as Kanye West. "Jesus Walks" could have been released by any of those Christian groups, and the world would have never heard the song. It would have only been made convenient to the Christian listener on a Christian station. Ask any local high school students to name one song performed by a Christian rap group, and unfortunately, they probably could not. However, if you were to ask the teens in your youth group about Kanye West, the majority would know his songs verbatim. "Jesus Walks" got into places that we, as Christians, could never place ourselves. It was played in clubs; it was blared from the speakers of the smoked-filled Escalade on 20-inch rims; it seeped into deep, dark places – the places we never expected Jesus to be mentioned or heard of. It put Jesus in the presence of whores with demons and evil tax collectors. This song wasn't made to be played in the temple; its design is not to strengthen the church, but to provoke the lost soul. "Jesus Walks" has the same effect on many Christians today as Jesus did when the Pharisees saw Him interacting with sinners. So my response is the same as Jesus' – He did not come to heal those who are whole but to heal the sick.

Maybe we are offended because we think that West used Jesus, a controversial figure, for his own selfish gain. Easter was the season; *The Passion of the Christ* was the movie; what better time to release a song called "Jesus Walks"? Maybe he knew that he could cash in on a Christian market that had been softened to support anything that promoted Jesus. Paul says in his letter to the Philippians,

> *"It is true that some preach Christ out of envy and rivalry, but others out of goodwill. The latter do so in love, knowing that I am put here for the defense of the gospel. The former preach Christ out of selfish ambition, not sincerely, supposing that they can stir up trouble for me while I am in chains. But what does it matter? The important thing is*

that in every way, whether from false motives or true, Christ is
preached. And because of this I rejoice..." (Philippians 1:15-18)

Whether we are talking about Kanye West or a money hungry preacher who only uses the gospel to cash in on God's people, Christ is still preached. Whether Kanye West does it for selfish gain or because he truly loves the Lord, Christ is still preached. Regardless of the motives, at the end of the day a soul is potentially saved. God will judge his motives.

Permission to Speak to Hip Hop

As previously discussed, Ezra was allowed to rebuild God's kingdom with the permission of a gentile king. In the same fashion, God later raised up Nehemiah to continue the work. After having received the king's permission to return to Jerusalem to rebuild the walls, Nehemiah secures his expedition by requesting written authorization. The rebuilding of the city and its walls was done under the favor and protection of kings who did not "know" the God of Abraham, Isaac and Jacob.

"I also said to him, 'If it pleases the king, may I have letters to the
governors of Trans-Euphrates, so that they will provide me safe-conduct
until I arrive in Judah?'" (Nehemiah 2:7)

Also, we read in verse 9 that "…The king had also sent army officers and cavalry with me." As we desire to evangelize a culture where our Christian authority is not recognized, we too are in need of the king's letter and his horsemen. I can hear the sentiments of the church now – 'We're the head, not the tail;' 'We are above and not beneath;' 'We don't need any *rapper's* permission to reach this hip hop generation!' Please understand that who you are in your church does not translate over into hip hop culture, the same way it would not have for Nehemiah. Your church title does not have the same value or carry the same weight with youth who have been raised by this street culture. They don't value any of the accolades or accomplishments which qualify you as a spiritual giant. Regardless of the fact that Nehemiah was a mighty man of God and a prophet of the Lord, if he had showed up without the king's letters and horsemen, the governors of the land would have stopped him. With all of his heart's desires, he would not have gone any further in his attempt to build. This is why he asked for the king's protection in the first place. Nehemiah understood that a king's name will grant him access to places he would otherwise never be allowed to go. As we tread upon the foreign soil of hip hop culture, we cannot go under our own protection. "Jesus Walks" is a letter signed by Kanye West; we have his approval and his army.

With Whom Does Jesus Walk?

In the second verse of "Jesus Walks," Kanye West lists hustlers, murderers, drug dealers and even strippers as people with whom Jesus walks. A comment I often heard when people were debating this song was that Jesus *does not* walk with those kinds of people. Although Jesus may not walk with them in the sense that he is in agreement with their behavior, neither is he absent in their salvation process. One of the videos for the "Jesus Walks" pictures a young lady (presumably a prostitute), a gangbanger, and an alcoholic living on the streets. The young lady is walking quickly, almost running, from a client who is trying his best to get her attention. The gangbanger is escaping a haunting enemy, and the old drunk is stumbling to get away from the block. Each character is in a different place, but they are all headed in the same direction. They fight through crowds and traffic jams, climb fences, and finally make it to the altar during a church service. It has been a long, difficult road for each of them, but they finally make it. This epitomizes the phrase "Jesus walks

51

with me." Before any of them made it to the point of changing, imagine how many times they could actually look back and say, 'Yo, that had to be God!' That phrase alone has helped me to make Jesus relevant to many nonbelievers. People wonder, 'Why didn't I get shot in that last shootout?;' 'Why didn't I get AIDS a long time ago?;' and 'Why haven't I died from all the years of alcohol abuse?' God's mercy is there far before one actually says, 'OK, God, I give up. You can take me now.' God is not stuck in heavenly places, glued to his seat in glory. He's an active force in the process of one's life being changed. I personally know that prison was God's harness, his hedge of protection in my process of getting to know Him before I *knew* Him. You find yourself doing life the same way you've always done it, and then suddenly out of nowhere, He comes by and says, "Follow me." The very last thing in the world that I was looking for when I was imprisoned was Jesus. An old guy named B. Red witnessed to me my second day in the county jail and gave me a Bible. I read the Bible every day until I completed it, which took me about eight months. My roommate D. would even read the Bible out loud though neither of us was saved. We simply felt a true peace that would come while he read. I now identify that peace as God's presence in the room. After three years of reading that Bible every day, I finally came to the realization that God had been too good to me *not* to serve Him. It is the goodness of God that brings a sinner to repentance (Romans 2:4). That goodness exists before you come into a relationship with God. Jesus told the disciples, "You did not choose me, but I chose you..." (John 15:16) Although you haven't had time to make preparations, and you still have your same problems and unmentionables, yet "Jesus Walks" into your world and offers an invitation for change. Jesus was walking *with* me before He lived *in* me.

Conclusion

The song "Jesus Walks," in my opinion, caught the church by surprise. We did not know if it was a weapon of mass destruction for the Christian world, or if it was a gift from God. We didn't know whether to put it in the sanctuary or to hide it in the closet. Would it be used as a wedge to open the pearly gates to sin, or as an instrument to help us become more compassionate for the world? Personally, it forced me to pray. Initially the song blew me away, but after the emotional high, I knew I had to seek God's truth. Exactly what did God have to say about such a song as this? God didn't speak to me this time in the same way that He always had. Trying to keep an open mind, I was seeking for a word or a subtle confirmation, but this time it came in floods. I was looking for something simple from God, and He wrote me a book. "Jesus Walks" ignited a fire in me to save the lost and dying world of hip hop culture. Kanye West has given us the permission, so now we must go.

Kanye West has not been the last or even the most recent example of a secular artist presumably taking a stand for Jesus. Though the song "Jesus Walks" is several years old, the principles outlined in this chapter can be used with any song that blurs the lines between sacred and secular. I pray that, when the next opportunity presents itself, we will be prepared to move in as evangelists.

Chapter Four

WELL TALK: CREATING DIALOGUE IN THE HIP HOP COMMUNITY

John chapter 4, the story of the woman at the well, is the most profound example of evangelism that we witness in scripture. What Jesus accomplished in that one encounter with the Samaritan woman was enough to write an entire "how to" book on evangelism. Scripture says that "...he who wins souls is wise" (Proverbs 11:30), and Jesus displayed masterful witnessing techniques that are absolutely necessary if we as the church are going to be effective in witnessing to the world around us, including hip hop culture.

The Bible tells that Jesus "...left Judea and went back once more to Galilee. Now he had to go through Samaria." (John 4:3-4) Jews hated Samaritans so much that they would usually travel around their region, even though it would take them longer to reach their destinations. The only reason Jesus needed to go through Samaria was because he had an "appointment" with the Samaritan woman. He saw her even before she got to the well. As we will discuss later, He effectively "gets in her space."

He had to be the aggressor because she wasn't seeking to be saved, as was the woman with the issue of blood who knew she had a need and pursued Jesus herself. (Luke 8) The Samaritan woman was approaching the well as if it was an ordinary day in her world. What Jesus did was position himself in her place of necessity. Everybody had to come to the well at some point because everybody needed water. If I want to deal with a world that assumes it does not need or have the time to seek out a savior, I must position myself in a place they must come. This is what I call "digging a well" – purposely setting ourselves up in a place where those of the world will come in order to create an opportunity for evangelism. For example, in our prison fellowship, we had a "tithing bag" – a system we created to faithfully pay our tithes. When the Christian brothers in our fellowship had money sent in from home for canteen, they would take ten percent of it and buy things such as toothbrushes, t-shirts, food items, socks, envelopes, razors, etc. We had a lot of faithful brothers, so we accumulated lots of stuff. This bag was used to provide for anybody on the prison yard who didn't have outside family or support, which unfortunately was the case for many of the guys. We would give these things away free, not only to church brothers but to anyone who was in need. If nothing else made my room popular, the tithing bag did! I would give away what was available and always encouraged the guys to come to church. That canteen bag became our well, a place of necessity to which many unsaved guys travelled.

Digging a Well

What are some other 'wells' that we can use to position ourselves for evangelism? A well doesn't necessarily have to be a physical object or location; it can be a subject of interest. Discussing sports, fashion, politics, entertainment – any of these can create interaction with someone that could lead to a witnessing opportunity. Many would claim that sports *is* a place of necessity for men, so at some point, they will come to this 'well.' For example, making a statement comparing Kobe Bryant to Michael Jordan will surely invoke an immediate reaction. Even the bystander overhearing the conversation will be tempted to jump in, not knowing that they may be forming a connection with someone that can lead them to Christ. The objective is to create neutral ground; a place where the Christian and a secular audience will be drawn to without any suspicion from either side. I risk seeming stereotypical, but for women, a common 'well' would be fashion. For example, a young lady comes into the beauty salon. 'Girl, I love those shoes! Where did you get those?' Immediately, a contact is made and an opportunity is created. As Christians, we are responsible for creating these 'well' experiences, these conversations which are actually opportunities to mix and mingle with the unsaved world around us. If we don't create these moments, we may never be given the opportunity to offer the gospel of Jesus Christ.

Hip hop culture's place of necessity, or 'well,' would be music and entertainment. *Mary Mary*, a Christian singing group, has done an awesome job of digging a 'well' relating to hip hop culture. They have consistently created music which draws a secular hip hop audience just as much as it draws Christians. When *Mary Mary*'s music is played, a secular audience gravitates toward it. They have a song called "God In Me" which has received lots of air play on secular stations. The beat is hot; they used hip hop diction in creating the lyrics; and they use a voice enhancer called Autotune which is really popular in hip hop music. It's a device which makes the voice sound robotic, and many secular artists use it to enhance their voices. *Mary Mary* certainly doesn't *need* it to sound great, but they use it to relate or "dig a well." Now this song may be sandwiched in on the radio between songs like "Birthday Sex" and "Boyfriend Number Two," but *Mary Mary* is still a Christian group effectively reaching out to a secular world. Even the accompanying video features significant secular artists like Kanye West, Heavy D, Fonzworth Bentley and Common, to name a few.

Mary Mary's music makes it easy for the Christian to find common ground with the secular world. However, the church sometimes calls this "well" a place of compromise because it's found between the church and the streets. This presumptive judgment is one of the reasons why Jesus sent the disciples away and interacted with the woman at the well by himself. In many cases, the church judges prematurely, which is exactly what the disciples did later when they saw Jesus at the well. If *Mary Mary* is to be questioned because their ministry is one that crosses over into a secular world, then I would challenge you to study their entire body of work. Not only that, Yolanda Adams' song "Open My Heart," Donnie McClurkin's "We Fall Down," Smokey Norful's "I Need You Now," and Marvin Sapp's "Never Would Have Made It" all had great cross-over success on secular radio stations. What we may call compromise may be the starting point of transition.

Receiving From Their Hand

After positioning himself in her world and place of necessity, Jesus makes the ultimate power move and asks the woman to give him a drink. Jesus goes from placing himself at her well to an even more intimate place of receiving a drink from her hand. Here is where Jesus really breaks the animosity that's supposed to be there amongst enemies. In asking for this drink, Jesus releases a battering ram, crushing the partition that had always separated the two groups. Even the woman was taken aback by it and said, "You are a Jew and I am a Samaritan woman. How can you ask me for a drink?" (John 4:9) She knew what the Jews thought about Samaritans and knew what Jesus' attitude *should* be toward her. This stereotype is exactly what Jesus was ministering to; He was challenging the perception. With that subtle, but earth-shattering gesture, He was annihilating the perception that she wasn't accepted by him simply because of her race. The gesture also said, 'I will receive what you offer or have to give.' In trying to create an opening for her to receive him, Jesus knew he had to first show her that he was open to receive from her.

So, how does this relate to our approach in evangelizing hip hop culture? What does it mean to show up at Hip Hop's well and allow them to pour us a drink? First of all, remember that their perception is that the church hates their music, their fads, their style, and their culture in general. That must be challenged. By receiving a drink from them, we as the church are establishing that they have something to offer us, and that there's something we can receive from them, even though we're supposed to be enemies. The cup that we receive from their hands may be their expertise on the job, their wisdom or insight in business, their gifts and skills, or even their passionate ambition. In the case of younger teens who may not have a polished skill to offer, a simple technique is to find out what they excel in or are interested in and ask all the questions you can. Tap into whatever they may have to offer. Become inquisitive. Sit and take a drink from their cup. Another great technique is to mention a song Hip Hop offers that even we as Christians can appreciate and respect. For example, Ludacris has a song called "Runaway Love." The lyrics of this song give insight on the troublesome issues that many young girls experience, such as abuse and teenage pregnancy. Referring to this song while talking to some young ladies can create a 'well' opportunity because they already know the song and the artist and have opinions to offer about it. Just mentioning this song may provoke the same reaction as the Samaritan woman gave Jesus at the well because you're not *supposed* to be drinking from Hip Hop's cup. I do admit that it may be difficult to find songs that do not promote vulgar or explicit behavior, but there are some. I'm not suggesting that we should watch hours of MTV or BET. Conversations with those who are familiar with the music, even non-Christians, can help us find these hidden treasures.

Another important thing to remember is that it's not that Jesus couldn't have gotten the drink for himself. It was important that he receive it from her hands; this penetrated the heart. In our evangelism efforts we become so fixated on giving salvation, giving deliverance, or giving insight that we sometimes become pushy, know-it-alls. This makes it difficult for anyone to receive from us, even though we're offering the amazing gift of salvation.

Can't Always Bring the Church to the Well

Let's look back to scripture and take a closer look at why Jesus sent the disciples away during this period of interaction at the well. In the story, the disciples represent the church. If the disciples had remained at the well, the woman may have taken a detour and not approached the well. She was purposely coming to the well at a time of day when few people would be there. She was attempting to have the least amount of contact with people possible. Jesus seemingly disconnected his affiliation with the other disciples; it looked as if he was there all by himself. We can learn from this strategy. It may often be necessary that we dismantle our glory and all that is affiliated with it in order to create moments that the unsaved can comfortably move into. Paul said, "I have become all things to all men…" (I Cor. 9:22) In the absence of the disciples, Jesus was seemingly just a regular man, able to converse without judgment or expectation. There was no hostility present. The woman's first contact with him was unintimidating; only later did she come to know Him as Jesus, the Savior. Oftentimes, we are afraid to "step away" from our church affiliation because it is what gives us a title, position or merit. We have found a place of significance among our church family and feel more confident with that backing. However, the church can be very intimidating to someone who knows that he doesn't "measure up." Although we must always be rooted in the church, we will sometimes need to create a separation. Sometimes you cannot take church fellowship to the well with you. If you do, you may end up attracting more church people and jeopardizing the comfortable place you wanted to create. I know that Sister Mary is fire baptized and speaks in many tongues, but she may tend to make people feel a bit uncomfortable. I know that Brother Bobby knows a lot of the Word, but all of his scripture quoting tends to alienate those who are not familiar with Christian jargon. They are great brothers and sisters, but you may not wish to invite them to the cookout this time.

Friendship, then Fellowship

Let's look at this idea just a little further. After Jesus converted the woman, the disciples returned, and scripture lets us know that the disciples questioned his actions but didn't say anything. Had the disciples come back before the woman had been enlightened, they could have definitely hindered the process. Should the conclusion be that the church doesn't play a role? Definitely not! The goal should always be for people to ultimately get connected with a church in order to be discipled and grow in their relationship with God. However, we sometimes sabotage the mission because we become so anxious to hand them church fellowship. We know fellowship to be an essential part in our growth and accountability, but for many it can feel like an ambush and they may become reluctant to approach or converse with anyone. Many think of witnessing as getting people to come to their church but that is not always going to be the case. Jesus created a connection – gave of himself, his time, and attention. Many people will need to develop a relationship with us personally that will lead to their salvation. They may not get connected to a church initially, and that may go on for a season. We don't like to think of it this way, but sometimes the church comes second in the process of salvation, as it did with the Samaritan woman.

Transition to a Deeper Place

Looking back at how Jesus led the woman to salvation, we see that He positioned himself at the Samaritan woman's well, asked her for something to drink, and then eased into her personal issues concerning the men in her life. Jesus slowly advanced into a more personal place, knowing that that was where he wanted to go the entire time. Notice that Jesus was advancing and pushing his agenda, but his mission goes unnoticed by the woman. That's why Jesus told his disciples, when he sent them out to witness, to be wise as serpents yet harmless as doves. To some, this "digging a well" approach may look like compromise; however, Jesus' only motive was to take her from the well to the church. He was in no way leaving a door open for her to take him from the well to the streets. The reason it sometimes goes the wrong way for us is because we settle in at the well without asking the difficult questions or bringing up the difficult issues. Our 'well' conversation should be thought provoking and challenging. If these issues are never brought up, the well is of no use. It has, at that point, become a place of compromise. Jesus was talking about water, but the whole time, he had in mind all the men that had been in her life. I can create a well at work by talking about last night's football game and get everybody to gather around, but the entire time, I'm concerned with ministering to their alcohol or drug abuse. What Jesus did was illuminate the part of her that, without a doubt, needed deliverance. This was the area in which she could admit for herself that she was in need of a Savior. Receiving from her cup gave her confidence that she had something to offer, empowering her. However, Jesus was now addressing a deficient area of her life. These areas will sometimes be revealed to us by God, and other times we'll just know by observation, but this is the turning point where we as Christians enter into the open gates of their hearts and witness Jesus Christ. Just like the woman at the well, the world doesn't always realize the need for Jesus until confronted with the ugly truth of its own deficiencies. It's much like convincing someone who feels fine that he should go see a doctor. He goes to the doctor reluctantly and may even be argumentative when he gets there, but something changes when the doctor comes back with an x-ray to tell him that he is dying of cancer. Suddenly, room is made for the doctor's advice, his counsel and his direction. Why? Because he makes them face the truth. Now he needs the doctor. Once Jesus exposed her personal situation about men, the woman at the well wanted Jesus to go deeper. He could now lead her to salvation.

The Process of Revealing Christ

Finally, the truth of Jesus' identity was revealed to the woman. He had seemed, at first, just a regular man. She then questioned whether he was a prophet. Ultimately, she called him Savior! She had had no idea who he was before he sat down; it was through conversation that she received revelation which led to her salvation. Her revelation came quickly, but it may not always happen that way for everyone. The process that leads to a true revelation of Jesus Christ in someone's life may take multiple encounters over a long period of time. Are we really ready for that? We all know that, as Christians, we have been commissioned to witness, but let's be honest about the feelings some people have about it. Unfortunately, some have reduced witnessing down to simply giving a word and feeling that they have done their duty, whether it was received or not. They wipe the dust off their feet without even making an honest effort. What Jesus did in five minutes of scripture reading may take us a month or longer. Creating an opportunity to receive from their cup is one thing. Moving deeper in conversation with their personal issues is another. Leading them to a true revelation of Jesus Christ is yet another. What Jesus did at the well was a model for witnessing, but it may or may not always happen that exact way. I know that there are situations that will require a quick and aggressive word because God is prompting us to do so. The person may only have a month left to live, or may be someone we will never see again. In other cases, however, you may have to go back to the well several times before you can delve into the deeper issues in a person's life. Jesus worked on me for about two years before I finally had my revelation! The point of it all is that our efforts to evangelize may sometimes take a little more than just asking 'Have you ever received

Jesus Christ as your Lord and Savior?' In all that we do, we must continue until Christ is revealed.

The Samaritan woman at the well came to a point of salvation even though it seemed as though her meeting with Jesus had been a coincidence. However, Jesus had known that she was coming the entire time and had even seen the end of the process. The purpose of the well is to create the "feel" that all is normal, that by happenstance or coincidence Jesus enters into their lives. Just offering heaven or hell and asking people to choose is not usually an effective method. Trust in the process – Jesus did.

Chapter Five

PAYING CAESAR:

HONORING THE KING TO GAIN ACCESS TO HIS PEOPLE

"*They came to him and said, 'Teacher, we know you are a man of integrity. You aren't swayed by men, because you pay no attention to who they are; but you teach the way of God in accordance with the truth. Is it right to pay taxes to Caesar or not? Should we pay or shouldn't we?' But Jesus knew their hypocrisy. 'Why are you trying to trap me?' he asked. 'Bring me a denarius and let me look at it.' They brought the coin, and he asked them, 'Whose portrait is this? And whose inscription?' 'Caesar's,' they replied. Then Jesus said to them, 'Give to Caesar what is Caesar's and to God what is God's.' And they were amazed at him.*"

(Mark 12:14-17)

Rappers establish themselves as kings, and their fans respect them as such. As ambassadors representing an outside nation, we must understand that we are maneuvering on the inside of their kingdom and that we won't get far if we don't at least acknowledge and respect the kings of the hip hop community. They asked Jesus if it was lawful to give tribute to Caesar or not. This was, of course, a setup to see if Jesus would disrespect the king and, in doing so, cause an immediate backlash. If Jesus would have all-out disrespected Caesar, it would have caused a greater rift. At that point, communication would have been rejected, and it would have turned into an uproar. Hip Hop has "setup" questions too, trying at all costs to find reasons to be offended and end the conversation. Always remember, if the doors of communication close, it will become very difficult to witness, no matter how powerful your message is. What is important in evangelism is not only what you have to say but keeping the door open so that you can say it. "An offended brother is more unyielding than a fortified city." (Proverbs 18:19) Jesus humbled himself to the hierarchy of the king in their society in telling them to give to Caesar what belonged to him. In doing so, Jesus gave Caesar proper respect as the king and, therefore, was able to advance his mission.

An example of one of Hip Hop's setup questions would be, 'What do you think about Tupac? Do you think he's in heaven or hell?' This is one of those types of questions that could quickly determine if the conversation will continue or not. Whatever you do, don't send Tupac to hell. Remember, this is not the time to disrespect the king nor is it time to become the great debater. The streets know how the church is *supposed* to respond and are looking to use that as a reason to end the conversation. Instead of putting Tupac in heaven or hell, you can make several powerful points which will lead the conversation to greater depths. For instance, just mentioning how gifted Tupac was as an artist is always a great start, signifying that you share a mutual respect concerning his many talents. Point the conversation upward in appreciation. This approach will not be expected and can help keep the conversation open. A way to turn the conversation into something more personal would be to say something like, 'Tupac died a horrific, untimely death. I personally believe he missed the true call on his life.' Our purpose in life is something we're all supposed to know but are seldom challenged to answer. This would be a perfect time to bring it up. You can simply say, 'Tupac had an uncanny ability to rally people through his music and message. Had he harnessed his leadership abilities, I think he could have been a great pastor! What do you think your purpose is?' This opens the door for all sorts of responses, so just go with the flow. Before the conversation ends, plant a seed of spiritual significance about Tupac – something that they can't deny and will remain fixed in their memories. For example, Suge Knight, owner of Death Row Records, bailed Tupac out of prison on the condition that he would sign to his record label and commit to several albums. He was there to bond Tupac out of jail and he was there in the car when Tupac was shot to death. Tupac was forever indebted to Suge Knight for getting him out of prison, but who would have known the payment would be his life? The lesson you can discuss here is to be careful who you owe and what you owe. It may cost you more than what you are willing to pay.

In these examples, I didn't put Tupac in heaven nor did I put him in hell, but there were several spiritual truths, causing the listener to evaluate himself and Tupac. When his followers ask these types of setup questions, they are not saying, 'Hey, do you think Tupac went to hell?' What they actually want to know is, 'Hey, what do you think about me? Do I have a chance with God or will *I* go to hell?' Tupac and other rappers are the voices that the hip hop audience relates to and connects with. Please don't close heaven's door in their face. State the facts along with God's Word and let them come up with their own conclusion about Tupac. This, in turn, will help them evaluate themselves. Without being judgmental, I give Tupac credit, and the conversation can continue. Respect, respect, respect – this is a culture that demands respect. Whether you like them or not, respect them!

Chapter Six

KING DAVID, THE FIRST RAP STAR
TIES BETWEEN DAVID AND HIP HOP

I f there was any genre of music that would relate to the life of King David, it would have to be Hip Hop. David was a bigger-than-life superhero whose story gives an honest account in epic proportions of victory and defeat. Had David been born today, he would be a hip hop artist. At first, this suggestion may be seem far-fetched or even offensive, but a closer look at his life will reveal how closely it actually parallels.

David, the Warrior

First of all, David was a fighter, a warrior by nature. In his humble beginnings as a shepherd, he fought lions and bears. This was before his legacy as a warrior began with him killing the giant, Goliath. David literally stole the hearts of King Saul's men as a valiant soldier on the battlefield, refusing to go down in defeat. Women lined the streets, singing that Saul had killed 1,000 but that David had killed 10,000. David, the warrior king, unified Israel as a kingdom through fear, intimidation and military conquest. No other music cultivates this warrior-like ambition like Hip Hop does. It is raw, aggressive, and in-your-face by nature. Hip Hop is so war-like that two of its brightest young superstars (Tupac and Biggie) were literally murdered in the streets because of their own lyrics! It was a battle that was so intense that it split an entire nation in half, east coast versus west coast. Even in the early days, rappers waged wars of words against each other, dating back to Roxanne Shante vs. UTFO, to L.L. Cool J. vs. Kool Moe Dee, to Cypress Hill vs. Ice Cube. Rap battles have actually been a part of the fabric that has helped stitch the hip hop audience to the rappers themselves. In other genres of music, it is about performing your best; in rap music, your best is beating the rapper standing across from you. Unlike other genres of music, rappers don't have the luxury of being peers; they are opponents.

David, the Lyricist

Secondly, David was a poet/songwriter. Let's examine the context of some of his psalms which so closely relates to Hip Hop. Many of David's problems concerned an actual enemy who was trying to destroy him, so he expounded on thoughts of hopelessness, uncertainty concerning God, distrust, and revenge, hoping that God would ultimately deliver him from such terrible circumstances. This sounds exactly like the theme of many hip hop CDs. What does a man say when he's at war? What does he think when his life is on the line and the enemy is closing in? Examining David's psalms, you almost want to delete them for God, to protect His reputation for allowing David to feel this way. The type of psalm that I am speaking of is called an "imprecatory psalm," coming from the word "imprecate" which means "to invoke evil upon; curse."[1]

72

Listen to David speak of his enemy:

> *"...May his children be fatherless and his wife a widow. May his children be wandering beggars; may they be driven from their ruined homes. May a creditor seize all he has; may strangers plunder the fruits of his labor. May no one extend kindness to him or take pity on his fatherless children. May his descendants be cut off, their names blotted out from the next generation. May the iniquity of his fathers be remembered before the Lord; may the sin of his mother never be blotted out. May their sins always remain before the Lord, that he may cut off the memory of them from the earth..."*

(Psalm 109: 9-15)

What would this song sound like if it was equipped with a beat from Doctor Dre (a prominent hip-hop producer who helped birth gangster rap)? Would David be considered just as gangster as Tupac? I realize that these scriptures are in the Old Testament, and that we are now under a different dispensation of God – that God no longer allows us to handle or even think of our "enemies" in the same manner. However, these psalms represent the harsh reality of what David, a man of God, felt concerning his enemies. When the enemy catches *us* off guard, do we sound like 50 Cent or Donnie McClurkin? I'm not saying that God approves the fact that rappers curse and scream towards each other; I want to offer a different perspective.

David, the Gang Leader

Let's take a look at some of the men that David was affiliated with. While David was on the run from King Saul, scripture tells us that, "All those who were in distress or in debt or discontented gathered around him, and he became their leader..." (1 Samuel 22:2) "Distress," "in debt," and "discontented," – these are the words used to describe David's first loyal followers. These are the unlikely characters, the outcast, the least likely to succeed. David recruited the boys from the hood who had nothing to lose and were definitely not the cream of the crop. Sounds to me like David was affiliated with a gang that he later turned into glory. Again, Hip Hop can definitely relate to that. Although David was gifted and called by God, he dealt with what could be considered thugs or low-lifes.

David, the Dancer

Let's consider how David danced and worshipped. Scripture says that David danced until his clothing came off. His wife Michal was even embarrassed by the way he worshipped and danced. Whatever he was doing was definitely high energy, and for a king to do so seemed uncivilized. Scripture says that he "… danced with all of his might before the Lord…" (2 Samuel 6:14) Sounds to me like he was doing what we in the hip hop community would call "getting crunk." Crunk originated out of down south, hip hop music that arouses high energy, wild, and seemingly out-of-control movements. It's similar to what you might find at a heavy metal concert – pushing, shoving, and screaming, with almost total disregard for whoever may be with or around you. Looks like David was getting crunk all by himself! What type of music do you think would promote this type of praising and dancing?

David, the Womanizer

David also had issues with women. Being a womanizer and a man of great authority seem to go hand-in-hand, then and now. I'm not saying that Hip Hop has any more of a problem with this than other music genres, but this is yet another element establishing the connection hip hop culture would have with King David. There was Abigail, who actually interceded for her husband whom David was on his way to kill. Later, after her husband died, David took Abigail as his own. Then there was Michal who was promised to David by her father, King Saul. When King Saul wanted to kill David, he left, and the two were separated. Michal was given in marriage to another man. Once David became king himself, he literally went back and took Michal from her new husband. The man followed weeping, but to no avail. Then, of course, there's Bathsheba, a woman who was another man's wife. David took her, had sex with her, impregnated her, and later killed her husband on the battlefield. There were others, but these are the most well-known. David was on his way to kill Abigail's husband; he took Michal away from her husband; and he killed Bathsheba's husband. David's life depicts a king who had a strong position of authority but was often defeated by his own insatiable lust for women. I'm sure hip hop can relate.

David, the Rapper

There you have it – David was a warrior by nature; he had a crew of misfits and outlaws; his songs carried a vindictive spirit about revenge and hate concerning his enemies; his worship and dance was wild and out-of-control; his women and power went hand-in-hand. Think about what has been described. Would David be a jazz musician, a gospel quartet member, a blues performer, or an opera, country, or pop singer? Taking all into consideration, I am sure David would be a rapper! (Heavy metal would run a close second.) Some of these points may even seem a bit comical, but this example of David allows the church to understand that neither we, nor our greatest example, are as far away from street culture as some of us would like to believe. Keeping this in mind will ultimately help us to relate.

David, the Underdog

One other parallel I would like to point out is that David's success in life grew from the bottom up. This is important when attempting to connect with those who are influenced by the world of Hip Hop. David wasn't born in a palace; he was the youngest of his father's children, too young even to go to war; and he wasn't even considered when they were seeking a warrior valiant enough to face Goliath. When it came time to anoint a king, David was initially disregarded by his father. Even when he was promoted in Saul's army, it was only a set up to have him killed. Because scripture takes so much time in developing the character of David, we can study and observe as he climbs the ladder of success – as he advances from a man to a king, from fighting and hiding in the wilderness to having a palace of his own, and from being laughed at by Goliath to being the most feared warrior king of his time.

Rap music has been referred to as "gutter," "underground," or "basement," even by the artists themselves. Rap music is the theme music of the underdog. To go from having nothing at all to having everything in the world – this is Hip Hop's angle. It glories in the fact that its participants, like David, were the ones that came from the bottom, overlooked and disregarded by their peers and the general public. One of Hip Hop's premier rappers, Ludacris, sums it up in his song "Grew Up a Screw Up" describing his transition from poverty to riches. He reflects on how he went from eating fast food to fine dining and from a one-room apartment to a mansion. It's the struggle that hip hop culture loves so much. One of Hip Hop's favorite movies would be *8 Mile*. It's the story of Eminem, a white kid from the trailer parks of Detroit breaking through the rap scene against all odds and becoming one of the most respected rappers today.

Hip Hop embraces its ties to the lowly places, celebrating humble beginnings, poverty, shame and despair. We, as the church, are by all means seeking a way out of these predicaments and would rather disassociate and disconnect from these things all together. We're fighting to get to heaven or at least raise our lives to kingdom standards. So, as Hip Hop celebrates coming from the bottom-up, it seems as if we are looking at them from the top-down, standing over them in judgment. It's our job to remove this perception and follow Christ's example. Scripture says,

> *"Your attitude should be the same as that of Christ Jesus: Who, being in the very nature God, did not consider equality with God something to be grasped, but made himself nothing, taking the very nature of a servant, being made in human likeness."* (Philippians 2:5-7)

Jesus came down out of heaven to break the tension and animosity between God and man and to give mankind the understanding that God is not only looking over us as a judge but also walking with us as a friend and father. It is not an option; it is our obligation to "associate with people of low position." (Romans 12:16) There is absolutely nothing more effective in changing our top-down positioning than our own testimony. Knowing our story helps those with whom we are witnessing to relate to us, just as knowing David's has helped us. We can see his whole life and realize that he wasn't perfect, but he had God's grace, mercy and favor working on his behalf. Our testimony is always a great way of descending, or coming down out of heaven, to meet people face-to-face. Remember, if they only see us as the strong Christian men or women we have become, they see only the end result. Giving them a complete view of the course it took to achieve glory makes it easier for them to follow the same path. Many of our journeys began at the bottom, far away from God. Even if your past is filled with shortcomings, mistakes, and regression, that makes your story even more credible. Most importantly, you as the church figure, become flesh and blood just like those you are attempting to relate to. Never, ever forget that Jesus suffered a public crucifixion. He didn't die away from the crowds, hidden in a dungeon. He went before the people publicly – weakened, naked and powerless. Sometimes revealing our areas of weakness allows God to get the glory because such revelation represents truth. Even if your testimony isn't as juicy as bank robbery and prison, that's alright. Find every opportunity to be honest about your struggles. Find ways to be a real person. Rappers aren't the only ones whose stories started out from the bottom and progressed upward. Your testimony is the most powerful tool you have to establish transparency and authenticity with an audience that places the utmost value on these traits.

Chapter Seven

LOOKING FOR LEGION: BRINGING OUR HEAVEN TO THEIR HELL

'*W*hen Jesus got out of the boat, a man with an evil spirit came from the tombs to meet him. This man lived in the tombs, and no one could bind him anymore, not even with chains. For he had often been chained hand and foot, but he tore the chains apart and broke the irons on his feet. No one was strong enough to subdue him. Night and day among the tombs and in the hills he would cry out and cut himself with stones. When he saw Jesus from a distance, he ran and fell on his knees in front of him. He shouted at the top of his voice, "What do you want with me, Jesus, Son of the Most High God? Swear to God that you won't torment me! For Jesus had said to him, Come out of this man, you evil spirit."* (Mark 5:2-8)

"Legion" is not the guy that you casually invite to church a few times and then eventually, after you've worn him down, gives in and comes with you. No, Legion is the person who is not seeking God in any way, shape, or form, so your invitation is no good. He can't get to the church because he's bound by demons and addictions. He's so possessed that the locals don't call him by his name; they call him "crack head", "pimp", or "dope boy." Nobody could bind Legion, and after a while, no one sought to help him. He was out of sight and out of mind. Legion doesn't *come* to church; he's *found* by the church. Jesus took the power and the anointing of the church to him in the graveyard, making no apologies about being the Savior. Legion is found in prisons, homeless shelters, recovery centers, juvenile homes, etc. He's been locked away, and the church has the key to free him. Every church that's really seeking to make a difference must be connected to the worst case scenario the streets have to offer. A healed Legion represents true power in a ministry.

Legion, the Neighborhood Legend

After Jesus healed him, Legion asked Jesus if he could go with him, but Jesus said that he could not. Instead, Jesus asked him to go and tell his testimony. He didn't give Legion healing power or train him up in the Word to be an apostle. He simply healed the man and told him to tell others. Legion's testimony is just as effective as any miracle in drawing others. After all, he had received the greatest of all miracles – salvation. Everybody had known that he was crazy, living in the graveyard, but now, all of a sudden, he's in a right state of mind! Jesus was sending him back home to his region, back to all those who had witnessed his former condition, because, just as his affliction was legendary in the area, his deliverance would be even more legendary. Legion's story was a monument to the locals, showing that Jesus can heal any condition.

Legion would be a big mouth for the kingdom of God, and that's why Jesus had such confidence in sending him away alone. We as leaders in the church should hand Legion freedom, permission and opportunity to tell his story as Jesus did. His testimony will destroy the yokes of bondage. Those who come in contact with him will say, 'Man, I know Legion. If *he* can be saved, there must be a God!' Even if they don't believe in God initially, they'll believe in Legion's change which will eventually lead them to God. In fact, witnessing a change in Legion was what led me to be saved. My codefendant Shane and I were tried in our case, sentenced, and then separated for two years. Shane had been much more involved in street activity than I had been. However, he became saved not long after our arrest and was growing speedily in Christ. Eventually he was transferred, and we ended up in the same prison. I will never forget the first time I saw him after being separated for so long. I was just coming back from my labor crew job. When I saw him, I really could not believe my eyes! From the moment that I saw him, even before he had a chance to say a word, I knew that God was real. His very countenance had such a glow, and I knew that no one but Christ could create such a graceful look of peace, joy and contentment. It was like having an encounter with an angel. I couldn't believe God had taken Shane, a guy that I had looked up to for all the wrong reasons, and changed him completely! He gave a guy like me permission to be saved and gung ho for Jesus. His testimony was much more powerful than anything else that could have been used to save me. Legion's deliverance will lead a multitude like me and many others to Christ.

Developing Street Credibility

Contact with a Legion from the community also gives the church street credibility. He hands us the permission, the respect, the right and the authority to interact with others like him. His affiliation gives Christians access to an entire community of those who are in bondage.

81

Why do we need Legion? There's a case against the church as far as the streets are concerned. In rap music and street circles, there's always a story of how someone has been wronged or neglected by the church. With a combination of our own mismanagement and the devil being an accuser, our "name" isn't necessarily popular in the streets. As we approach, skepticism creates confrontation as opposed to conversation. This is why a connection to Legion is absolutely vital. I can't tell you how often I've been introduced to someone as 'Rick the Christian' or 'the preacher,' but then a disclaimer is added '...but he's cool' or 'He's good people.' I can almost see the words that are written in the back of their minds saying, 'If my friend is cool with Rick, then Rick must be okay.' David says "A good name is more desirable than great riches." (Prov. 22:1) This is so true and even more when you're talking about a culture in which reputation is everything. The streets are already talking about how the preacher's car is too nice, the church is taking everybody's money, all the deacons sleep with the women, and all church members are a bunch of hypocrites. Befriending Legion gives us a chance, a moment to state our case for our love for them through Christ; his friendship is a wedge in the door that would normally be slammed shut in our faces. His connection with us allows them to meet our true characters. Legion needs our healing and we need his allegiance so that a community which sits in darkness may be healed.

Chapter Eight

GOLIATH, THE GIANT SLAVE: MAKING HIP HOP SERVE US

D avid began his illustrious career as a warrior when he faced Goliath, the Philistine giant. Later, as a warrior king, David dealt with the Philistines time and time again. They were a constant threat – always present, always near. They were enemies, allies or servants to David at different times during his reign. He was even retired by the Philistines, almost losing his life during his last recorded battle. Overcoming Goliath did not bring an end to the Philistines' influence, but it did mean that there was a shift in power and position. Goliath had made this proposition before he fought David, "If he is able to fight and kill me, we will become your subjects; but if I overcome him and kill him, you will become our subjects and serve us." (1 Samuel 17:9) David's triumphant victory immediately made him and the children of Israel rulers instead of slaves. In that battle alone, there was a shift in power.

It is undeniable that Hip Hop has become an ever present influence in our society and even in our churches and homes. I often hear parents and ministers complain about how it is destroying our youth. These adults feel powerless, much like the Israelites, in their ability to fight against the giants of the hip hop world. We, like David, need to seek to create a power shift. The key to overcoming the influence of these giants is to address them "face to face," exposing the truth of their identities. Our teenagers often have an unbalanced view of hip hop artists. We must arm ourselves with the truth and dismantle the images to which they submit. We need to make these idols serve us, just as David did with Goliath.

Exposing the Truth about Rappers

What exactly am I proposing? We've already discussed how many artists are not the "gangsters" that they claim to be in their lyrics. Although they embellish their stories in their lyrics, they are much more honest in their books and magazine interviews. They often give insight about how hard they've fought to get *out* of the streets and pursue their careers. However, they can still rap about being on the streets without seeming like contradictions because much of their listening audience will not pick up their books and read them. As parents and youth ministers, we need to educate ourselves about these artists so that we can discuss the real truth with our teenagers.

I went to the theater to see 50 Cent's movie, *Get Rich or Die Trying*, based on his life story. I knew that most teens were probably going to see it, so I made an effort to see it as well. To my surprise, whether done intentionally or not, this movie actually sent out a strong message *against* street hustling and dealing. It included several powerful scenarios that dealt with the harsh realities of the drug game. In the beginning of the movie, 50 Cent gets shot nine times, including a shot to his face.

Later, his mother (a hustler herself) was murdered by being burned to death. He had a friend was shot and was paralyzed, and 50 Cent himself was thrown in jail and almost killed while he was there.

After 50 completed his time in prison, he decided to leave the drug game behind, but there was only one problem. On the day of his release, both his music manager, whom he had met while in prison, and his boss in the drug game showed up to take him home. He struggled in deciding with whom to go, but ultimately chose his music manager so he could follow his dreams and do music. The drug dealing kingpin, however, haunted him from the time he got out of prison until the end of the movie.

Rappers Preach, Their Audience Listens

I don't know what 50 Cent's purpose was in doing such a movie. It may have been for self-glorification, but that doesn't matter. 50 actually preached to the at-risk teenager who has great passion to follow his dreams but has present circumstances fighting against his destiny. In his own words, 50 gives lessons about the sacrifice and courage it takes to leave the only life you've ever known behind. He teaches that a good work ethic is a process that will, ultimately, beat out the instant gratification of hustling. He also shows how the 'old man' of your past will never stop pursuing you as you pursue your dreams. At the end of the movie, the drug-dealing kingpin showed up again at one of 50's shows and was shot and killed by his manager. 50 then walks onto the stage to perform for a screaming crowd that helps to propel his future to a place that even he could never have imagined. The lesson here is that the 'old man' and his affiliates must "die" before you can fully live out what you have been called to do here on earth.

When I speak of watching 50 Cent's movie, I'm using it as example of how we can remain relevant to those we are trying to reach. Understand that I am in no way suggesting that you plan an event to take your youth group to see a movie like this. However, as parents and youth workers, we will always have a mix of young people that we deal with. Our responsibility is to effectively minister to all of them. Some have already developed a passion and discipline that comes with a mature Christian walk. These young people will be more inclined to safeguard themselves from seeing a move like this. We should definitely encourage that. On the other hand, there are those who may not be saved or are lukewarm in their Christian walk. This group may not even think twice about viewing 50 Cent's movie. Instead of throwing shame on them, we need to engage them in conversation. This is how we make Hip Hop serve us. 50 Cent preached a message in their language, in terms that we could never preach. If we see the movie or educate ourselves about it, we can then interpret, pull out and expound messages that they may miss. Many would say that letting them see the movie is dangerous but what is more dangerous is that they see the movie without us. Using the movie *Get Rich or Die Trying* is only one example of the kinds of ways we can make Hip Hop serve us.

Small Rock, Big Giant: Bringing Hip Hop Down to Size

In hip hop culture, image is everything, and the image is always far better or far worse than is the actual person. Remember that the devil is the father of all lies. Scripture tells us,

> *"How art thou fallen from heaven, O Lucifer, son of the morning! How art thou cut down to the ground, which didst weaken the nation...They that see thee shall narrowly look upon thee, saying, Is this the man that*

made the earth to tremble, that did shake kingdoms; That made the world as a wilderness, and destroyed the cities thereof; that opened not the house of his prisoners." (Isaiah 14:12, KJV)

Exposing the enemy is the key to confronting and controlling Hip Hop. In his music, 50 Cent portrays himself as a killer and an intimidator, destroying the lives and careers of his opposition. In examining his life, however, one realizes that he is an ambitious entrepreneur who makes ingenious business maneuvers. In his book "From Pieces to Weight," he says,

> "*Truth is, there's no such thing as a 'gangsta rapper,' because no one can be a 'gangsta' and a 'rapper' at the same time. A rapper can have gangsta ties, he can know gangstas, but he can't be a gangsta. He has to be an artist if he's going to be an artist. I was still trying to figure out which I was going to be. It's like I had a microphone in one hand and my Ruger [a gun] in the other...*"[1]

He later says,

> "*A gangsta will always side up with a weak party who needs them for strength. That's because most gangstas haven't developed their talents. Instead, they take advantage of people who have talent through fear. The fear factor allows a weak artist to hang with gangstas, to make the stories he puts on a record sound real. If someone's whole gangsta backstory is a lie, he's going to try to make it look like it's real by standing next to someone who may have had those experiences. But that doesn't mean you're down with gangstas. That just means you're getting extorted by gangstas.*"[2]

This is 50 Cent's confession about his very own culture and the culture of most of the rappers in the game. Now, you won't hear this in his music, but you can read it in his book. That's where we come in. All too often, our kids try to live the life that rappers promote; however, they miss the fact that these artists don't even want to live that lifestyle themselves. We, as the educated audience, must become more aggressive at exposing this.

As a parent, youth leader, or simply a concerned friend, begin to educate yourself about the popular artists your teenagers listen to. For example, Jay-Z, Lil Wayne, and 50 Cent are all multimillionaire entrepreneurs. Let's be honest, it is impossible to hustle on the block and do a tour in Tokyo at the same time! These guys aren't street hustlers, they're entertainers!!! Sort of like fake wrestlers. These are business men with tattoos and bandanas; they are money-making machines, not killers. It sounds pretty obvious to us that these men are not still in the drug game, but your 15 year old may not have thought of it this way. We hesitate, either because of fear or lack of knowledge, to touch on these stories, so rappers take full advantage and are allowed to push this false image. Remember Goliath was powerful and in control only because he wasn't confronted. How long would the Israelites have allowed the Philistines to enslave them if David had not exposed Goliath's image for what it was? How long will our children stay enslaved by the giants of Hip Hop before we expose their false images? The monster image of these artists is growing only because we have yet to dismantle it. We look at these artists and we run; we hear their raps and are petrified. Go towards Goliath and make the giant serve us!

Chapter Nine

CONNECTED, BUT NOT MARRIED TO HIP HOP CULTURE

Being proactive and drawing closer to hip hop culture is necessary for evangelism; however, we must be careful not to cross the line of compromise. The only thing worse than running away from Hip Hop in total separation is getting too close, leaving no division or distinction at all. Our goal should be to establish an effective connection to the culture while maintaining a healthy separation from its negative influences. In other words, we are not to come in total agreement with all that the culture offers. Instead, we confront the lifestyle, address the real issues, and provoke change. In marriage, there is a give and take, a compromise of sorts. In our evangelistic efforts, it is a great temptation to enter into the same type of agreement, giving Christ yet taking too much of hip hop. It always bothers me when I leave a youth event feeling as though we've simply mimicked the caricatures of hip hop gods. It also baffles me when a Christian rap artist can do an entire show and not even smile, wearing the same stone face as secular hip hop artists. If we're not careful, not only will this tough hip hop demeanor enter into the church but so will its attitude and spirit. It doesn't barge its way in. It comes in through "marriage," a covenant that we've agreed upon. As a result, we find ourselves with "...a form of godliness..." (2 Timothy 3:5)

Compromise Leads to Destruction

Solomon was a king surrounded by nations that gave him all sorts of gifts, lavish materials, and even concubines. Solomon's connection, or allegiance, with these other kingdoms was not the compromise. The compromise happened as a result of Solomon marrying these strange women who worshipped false gods. He eventually made houses for their gods and led the children of Israel into idol worship. The devil was after Solomon's worship and what better way to do this than to marry him into it.

Samson was another mighty man of God whose compromise with the enemy ultimately altered his purpose and mission. Instead of remaining true to his call, he fell in love with the enemy, whose sole mission was to strip him of his strength. Delilah was a Philistine who worshipped the false god Dagon. Samson was there to deliver the Israelites from the affliction of the Philistines. Instead, he was stripped of his power through compromise and handed the children of Israel over again to a false god.

Ahab was another king of Israel who God truly wanted to use, but Ahab married Jezebel, the evil force behind idol worship. She completely disqualified Ahab as a ruling king and used his name to push her own agenda. Once again, the children of Israel were intertwined with idolatry. These are examples of what happens when we get too close. We must be careful not to be so "hip" that we lose "holy" in the process —this is the devil's ultimate plan.

Daniel, on the other hand, represented a man of God ministering in a foreign nation who never compromised his commitment, or marriage, to God's will. He never lost sight of his purpose or influence while living in the dominion of gentile kings. He kept his gift of interpreting dreams, and God established him as a prophet, an intercessor, and a man of wisdom, intelligence, and understanding.

Appetite Under Attack

Daniel and his friends were aggressively challenged by the enemy to compromise their relationship with God. The first challenge to their covenant is found in Daniel 1. They were in training for three years before they would be presented to the king to work in his administration. The challenge came when they were asked to accept the king's royal food and wine. This food was fit for royalty and would seemingly offer the best results in health, but Daniel knew that that type of food violated his covenant with God and refused it, saying that he would only eat vegetables and drink water. This may seem like a small issue. However, in offering the food, the devil was seeking to create an appetite or an opening in Daniel and the others. He knows that if he can create an appetite, then he can entertain, offer and negotiate. Think about it: no one ever starts out doing "it," whatever "it" may be. "It" is always negotiated through smaller things. We work ourselves up to "it." The royal food was a test of whether Daniel would be willing to make an exchange. Once we feast at the enemy's table, we enter into agreement that can set the stage for more to be offered. It is no surprise that the initial violation of Samson's covenant came when he ate honey from a dead carcass, breaking his Nazarite vow. The devil knew that if he could get Samson to eat, then he could eventually get him to allow his hair to be cut. Adam also forsook his agreement with God by eating the fruit in the garden. And let's not forget about Esau forfeiting his entire birthright for a bowl of soup. Be careful not to receive what the enemy offers in exchange for what God has promised.

Worship Under Attack

Later in Daniel 3, the Hebrew boys had another test concerning their covenant with God. It was a test of their worship. King Nebuchadnezzar had made a golden image that was ninety feet high and nine feet wide. The announcement was made that, anytime one heard the instruments playing music, he was to fall down and worship the image that the king had set up. This colossal golden figure, which could not be ignored, was supposed to replace the God of the Hebrew men. Notice that the cue to worship the idol was music. Music and images go hand-in-hand. We sometimes are not even aware that we are bowing as the devil wheels the golden image onto the screens of our imagination. (Consider hip hop music and its videos) Worship is an essential part of our relationship with God. After all, the first two commandments deal with worship and false idols. In hearing the music and seeing the idol, the Hebrew boys did not bow and were, of course, thrown into the fiery furnace. As we interact with an ungodly culture, we have to always be aware of how the enemy will try to steal our worship away from God. Can we take the same bold stance as the Hebrew boys did?

Prayer Under Attack

Daniel 6 tells us how Daniel's commitment to God is once again tested. A decree was signed by the king that no one should pray to any god or man except King Darius for thirty days. The penalty would be that they would be thrown into the lion's den. Daniel was committed to praying to God three times a day with his window open and did not change this habit because of the decree. He knew that if he could not pray to God, he would become totally ineffective. Daniel understood that prayer was his lifeline. His communication, devotion, and intercession were all being attacked. Again, we see the enemy trying to break down another component in the godly relationship that exists in order to destroy it and exchange it for an alternative.

The Signs of Compromise

We've seen how the devil seeks to enter in through appetite (what we receive), worship, and our prayer life. An analysis of all three of these plays such a vital part in determining if we're really ministering to a culture or if we've become married to it. The enemy first sought to create an appetite in Daniel's flesh. In dealing with hip hop culture, we must be careful that, as we are connecting and finding common ground, we don't find ourselves seated at their table full of delicacies and desserts that cater to our flesh. In attempts to make us drunken gluttons from the world's goods, the devil is hoping that we will enter into agreement with his dubious agenda.

The devil's next move was to attempt to break into their place of worship. Hip Hop introduces their gods through music and videos. Are you watching more MTV, BET or TBN? Do you listen to more and more secular Hip Hop, or are you influenced and inspired by Christian artists? These are questions that you must continually ask yourself in order to evaluate how the enemy is affecting your worship.

Eventually, as with Daniel, there will be an all-out attack on your commitment and diligence in prayer. Is your prayer life thriving? Are you interceding for the culture with fervor and zeal, or have you sided with the enemy who has silenced your prayer life? If we cut off our line of communication with God, we'll have no power to effectively interact in this foreign land of hip hop.

These three areas must become focus areas for all of us who are involved in evangelizing Hip Hop. If any one of these areas is compromised, we are too close to marriage with the culture. Sometimes we don't even notice that we have gotten so close, and we do what Samson did after Delilah cut his hair. He thought he would break loose from the bonds the same way he had always done, but this time he couldn't. He had forfeited his strength, power and purpose, and it was too late. It was obvious that he was breaking covenant all throughout the story. It was a slow fade that led to his utter destruction. The sad part is that, though he regained his strength and relationship with God by the end of the story, he still died under the enemy's plan to destroy him and left a nation in the rubble of shame and affliction.

A Healthy Separation

Daniel and his Hebrew friends were under the rule of foreign nations, so they couldn't just give up one day and say, 'That's it. We're tired. We're going home.' The same is true for us at our jobs or our children at school; we have to deal with a secular king and his rule. It's not so simple as saying that we won't become intertwined or connected with the secular world. Because you *are* connected to the secular world, God's covenant with you should be firm and consistent. If the enemy cannot destroy you, he will attempt to make you ineffective. Ministry that maintains a healthy separation from the culture allows us to reach in to our youth in order to pull them out. Marriage to the culture grabs us and pulls us into a place where we dismiss the original mission. As Christians who are evangelizing the culture, we have to remain in a safe place of ministry and not be drawn into compromise.

Chapter Ten

OUR WISDOM, THEIR STRENGTH: HELPING OUR YOUTH WIN THEIR WAR

There was a battle between the Philistines and Israel during King David's reign. Scripture says that,

"...David went down with his men to fight against the Philistines, and he became exhausted. And Ishbi-Benob, one of the descendants of Rapha, whose bronze spearhead weighed three hundred shekels and who was armed with a new sword, said he would kill David. But Abishai son of Zeruiah came to David's rescue; he struck the Philistine down and killed him. Then David's men swore to him, saying, "Never again will you go out with us to battle, so that the lamp of Israel will not be extinguished."*

(2 Samuel 21:15-17)

This was one of David's last battles in which Abishai, a younger warrior, saved his life. David had been a mighty warrior, legendary for his courage and success in battle. However, he was now older. His time had passed, and he was getting in the way. At some point, leaders in the church must discern when it may be time to pass the torch to the next generation. David retired and encouraged his men from the sidelines to fight new giants. As an older, mature crowd, are we standing in the way of victory or are we setting the stage for a new era of warfare?

Raising Your Deliverer

Samson's parents were told before he was even born that his purpose was to deliver God's children from the vices of the Philistines. This notice came to the parents, but it was specifically for their son. His parents could have looked at the Philistine army and said, 'No way, not my child!' They could have gotten in the way, fearful of the consequences that such a call would have on their child. However, Samson's parents knew that to deny Samson this call would be denying their own deliverance. The questions to modern-day parents are this: Could you be Samson's mother? Could you be Samson's father and prepare your child for such a call? Could you mentor or raise a modern-day David? Where there is a Philistine, there has to be a Samson; where there is a Goliath, there has to be a David.

Handing Our Children A Sword

I often talk to parents who, although they don't say it directly, have grown weary and approach opposition from a position of fear instead of faith. They, in turn, place the same perspective in their child's mind. When one drives past the local high school or community hang-out or listens to the first five minutes of the news, it is like looking into the land of giants and saying, 'There's no way. Let's just settle right here and leave them alone.' The church all too often relates to Hip Hop with this same fear. Instead of being proactive, we do the next best thing – we become protective. We pray that gangs would leave our communities not realizing that, all the while, the change agents for stopping the gangs (our children) are at home with us looking out the window.

When I speak to people about handing their children a sword and letting them fight their own war, many feel that I'm asking them to let their child stand alone in the middle of a shootout. That would be crazy, and that's not what I'm promoting – I promise. What I will share next is probably the most vital information to the church and parents about helping this generation win their war. They need a way to fight off the temptations of the enemy and witness to their peers without being influenced themselves. Our best strategy is to help them develop the gifts they were given. David's ability as a musician is what got him into the palace and into the presence of the king. (1 Samuel 16) Samson's gift was Samson's fight; there's a direct correlation. Whether poetry writing, singing, dancing, sports, playing an instrument, or even academics – their strengths need to be encouraged as an integral part of their lives. When we don't understand their strengths, tap into their gifts, or encourage the genius in our children, we take away their ability to beat or fight off the constant attack of the enemy. They struggle to find out what their fight or their gift is because we do not encourage its development. Many may know their gift or fight but feel that we won't offer the space or allow it to be developed in our church. Their gifts may not be the same things which made *us* happy or gave *us* victory. Remember, David could not wear King Saul's armor; it didn't fit. God is consistent, but ever-changing. He creatively develops gifts in each generation that are appropriate for their challenges.

Their Gift is Their Fight

An example of how teenagers' gifts can help them fight against the temptations of this world is exemplified in the documentary *Rize*. This is a video about the youth in South Central California who have been brought up in gang-infested neighborhoods of crime and violence. These inner city youth, despite their living situations, have come up with their very own dance style that has taken the hip hop world by storm. It all began with a clown group that was started by a guy named Thomas Johnson, or "Tommy the Clown." Tommy and his entourage would dress up like clowns and perform at birthday parties and events for the children in the neighborhood. The clown dancing birthed what is now called "krumping" – lightning fast and unpredictable jerking motions involving the entire body. Different clown groups (literally hundreds) came forth with their own twist to the dance and competitions began. What started out in the streets of Compton made it all the way to the Staples Center in Los Angeles where two of the most popular groups squared off. Hearing the music and watching the dancers gyrate back and forth in circles, one might say that the dance moves were offensive, wild and crazy. Some might even think that these kids are under some type of demonic influence. As I watched the video, I was captivated by the dance moves but even more by the kids' stories. One had been shot by his grandfather and said that, as a child, he had had to literally go into a crack house to get his mother. Another boy's father had committed suicide when he was younger. Still another's father was in a gang, and the boy was now being recruited by a gang as well. Another kid's mother gave testimony of how she had been in a gang and on drugs and how her son had raised his little brothers and sisters. The testimonies were touching, but a common thread throughout their stories was gang influence. Remember, this is an

100

area where it is understood that, if you grow up and become of age in a certain 'hood,' you are in a gang. What was said most often in their testimonies was that, if the kids weren't dancing, they would probably be active gang members. These kids had actually tapped into their 'fight'! Their dancing became for them an alternative to gang affiliation. See, we would look at the video and say, 'Man, they shouldn't dance like that,' but their parents are saying, 'I thank God that they are dancing because, if they were not *dancing* against one another, they would probably be *shooting* at one another.'

Please understand that I'm not trying to say that church youth groups across the country should adopt these dances. The key here is to understand the principle. The dance helped these kids create their own subculture, and that has helped them resist, even fight off, the influence of gang culture. Their dance was a matter of life and death, not just a gift. What I thought was even more interesting was that, towards the end of the documentary, several of the dancers who were featured were also active in their local church. Be careful when you tell him that he's not allowed to rap or she cannot dance. Quite naturally, all that we do must be Christ-centered, but maybe God is expanding our view on what may be considered a gift. If *we* don't accept these youth, they will find a place to be accepted. The world will put them on stage and exchange their gifts for their souls.

A caution to spiritual fathers and leaders

David was an explosion of youthfulness, a cannonball of fury moving with fearless intentions of attack and initiative. While He became a terror to the enemy, in truth, David was more of a threat to the leaders over him. His fanatical ambition in battle exposed how outdated, stagnant, and ineffective the traditional methods of leadership had been against this particular giant. Although this type of character would be great in any army and would only help advance the kingdom, many "Davids" in today's churches die from what would be considered friendly fire. Why? Well, in order to lead David, you yourself must be led by God. It is much easier to tell David "no" or "stop" than it is to seek God concerning his direction. If the modern day David goes forth and has success, many, like Saul, are afraid that they will become witnesses to an awesome move of God which doesn't require yesterday's glory. The reality is that David is not there to steal or take. He's really looking to be fathered. An insecure father, however, will end up making David the villain. In order to protect their honor and reputation, the old regime becomes defensive and insecure, plotting to remove David completely from the picture. Jesus ran into the same issue. When He was born, there was supposed to be a spiritual structure in place that would propel him into ministry, but as we see in scripture, Jesus had to create a movement outside of the established religious tradition. The leaders at that time were not led by God and could never give Jesus guidance or direction, though they claimed to be spiritual. The Pharisees knew that, as long as Jesus remained, their ministry seemed incompetent and ineffective by comparison. Can you imagine the Pharisees flexing their spiritual prowess, memorizing entire passages of the Torah, while Jesus was raising the dead, giving sight to the blind and casting out demons? The killing of Jesus did not heal the ills of a nation in need, but it put the church back at ease, back in the order of predictability and contentment, back under the power of the devil himself. Many "Davids" are either on the run from church or have died as a result of spiritual fathers who did not know how to raise him. Unfortunately, this happens all too often in many of our churches.

David, whether an ambitious man or woman of God, may employ nontraditional methods that will challenge the church's views of what can be used by God. The question for his leaders is whether they will pray for God's guidance or lead an assault against a potential move of God.

To the leader who has grown weary in battle:

I want to speak briefly to those of you who have been dedicated ministers but are becoming tired in the fight. As a youth minister and a brother who has done prison ministry for several years, watching guys go in and come out, I understand how quickly you can start to question whether anybody is listening, whether anybody will truly be saved. Sometimes hopelessness can set in, and that alone can make you want to quit. We all remember Elijah the prophet confronting false prophets and idol worship during his time. Scripture tells us that Elijah felt overwhelmed – that there was no one who was on his side, none who would listen, and no one who would be saved. To say the least, Elijah was burnt out. Here's some helpful advice when you have fought your battle and are tired and fatigued – put down your sword and pick up your oil. Stop fighting and start anointing. Every Elijah needs to find his Elisha. This isn't always an easy task. You need to find someone who wants what you have – the one who desperately longs for that double portion. He is not just under the sound of your voice but under your hands, looking to be raised by you. You can pour into him because he is open to receive.

This principle of duplicating yourself in ministry is so important. If you don't embrace this principle, you may become bitter, feeling more and more often that those you are ministering to aren't grasping what you are saying. Even Jesus experienced this. His strategy was to pull his disciples away from the multitudes so that he could really pour into them.

He knew that he needed to develop others for ministry, and that this would allow him to extend and do more than what he could do alone. He also needed to prepare his disciples for the time that he would no longer be with them in ministry. Also, after Elijah runs and hides in a cave because of his frustration, God tells him,

> *"Also, anoint Jehu son of Nimshi king over Israel, and anoint Elisha son of Shaphat from Abel Meholah to succeed you as prophet. Jehu will put to death any who escape the sword of Hazael, and Elisha will put to death any who escape the sword of Jehu."* (1 Kings 19:16-17)

The lesson learned from Elijah – he whom you anoint will get to those who are out of your reach.

To the parent who has grown weary in battle:

I would also like to speak to those parents who are trying to fight their child's battle for him. I'm sure you often find yourself weary and fatigued as well. Referring back to the story of David, his men told him, "Never again will you go out with us to battle, so that the lamp of Israel will not be extinguished." (2 Samuel 21:17) This is the greatest and most difficult advice I can give to any parent who is dying, trying to fight their child's war. David's men knew and understood his worth to the nation, and the devil understood it as well. If David were to stay in the battle and die by a Philistine sword, not only would it kill David, but it would also annihilate the morale of David's men. Mother, what happens when you "die" because you won't put down your sword? What will happen to your child if he can't fight for himself?

When I started getting into trouble in school and with the law, my mother began to have health issues. I wouldn't say that what was going on with me was the only factor, but I know that it definitely contributed. She started having issues with ulcers and anxiety attacks. Looking back, I can see that the devil was not only after me; he was after my mother, knowing that she was the source, the strength, and the glue that kept our household in order. She was our light. If the devil had succeeded in destroying my mother, I wouldn't be where I am today.

Matthew 8 tells us the story of a Centurion, a Roman captain over a hundred men, whose servant was sick and dying. He approached Jesus about the issue, and Jesus said that he would come and heal the servant. The Centurion replied by saying, "Lord, I do not deserve to have you come under my roof. But just say the word, and my servant will be healed." (Matthew 8:8) The Centurion understood the power that comes from a word spoken by God. Once David retired from the battlefield, he had to exercise what the Centurion had done in this similar situation. He had to trust and have faith that, although he couldn't be there to put out every fire, God's word superseded his presence and that God's word was the power and authority needed to win the war. In turn, David could have peace knowing that God would fight with his men. Mothers especially, but fathers as well, are running to try to "save" their child (not always a *young* child) in every situation, from the principal's office to the jailhouse and everywhere between. You must discern when your presence is necessary or when you need to sit down and believe the word that God has sent out of heaven. Remember, if you die on your way to bail him out again, the light goes out for everyone. I now thank God that, with a $325,000 bond, my mother could not run down to the jailhouse and get me out of prison. She, instead, developed a trust in God and sent His Word to come get me. Will you do the same?

To the Church concerning our youth:

If we're really going to help our younger generation avoid negative influences and minister to those in Hip Hop culture, we have to do better when it comes to partnering with other churches. Our church's old, bitter rivalry with the church down the street is actually keeping our children from banding together as an army of Christian young people. As we send our children into public schools and community events, they need to be in connection with as many Christians in their area as possible. It's not easy to stand on Godly convictions when it seems as if you are alone in your school. Let's be honest, oftentimes the undercurrent of our old church rivalries stamps out the connection and fellowship that our young people could have with churches that are near. Is the church just as gangster and territorial as the streets? Picture this scene for just a moment – two Christians attend different churches within a mile of each other. Both are dedicated members and absolutely love their church. Each has their church's logo keychain, license plate, sun visor, sweatpants, etc. Everything that bears the church's emblem, they have it. When these two individuals approach one another, do they represent individual churches or do they represent the unified body of Christ? This display of church pride looks innocent, and oftentimes is, but when it is mixed with corrupted communication and wrong attitudes, an encounter can be just as lethal as throwing up gang signs. We are often so aggressive and competitive in marking our territory for the expansion of the "kingdom" that we disregard, bully, and offend whoever is standing in the way, even fellow Christians and churches. Many of our neighborhoods, especially in the African-American communities, are torn and separated as they stand between our churches' gang war of words. Life and death is in the power of the tongue, and for many of us, our mouth is a smoking gun aimed in the direction of a "rival" church. Does rap music and its influences get all of the blame for the great divide in our neighborhoods? Could we be the real gangsters in our communities? The streets' division will not be effectively overcome by the church's separation. Nor can we offer a real alternative when our own tendencies mirror those of street rivalries. It will take a united front of faith, manpower, and resources to win over the Goliath which threatens and intimidates the future of our youth. We've already discussed how divisive the world of Hip Hop can be. It is no surprise that Hip Hop and gang culture go hand in hand, but upon careful inspection, it also seems that gang culture and our churches have more in common than we would like to admit. Often, getting two pastors to come to a place of agreement can be just as difficult as getting gang leaders to call a truce.

In the Old Testament, the children of Israel were grouped into twelve separate tribes. God told Moses,

> *"Make two trumpets of hammered silver, and use them for calling the community together and for having the camps set out...When you go into battle in your own land against an enemy who is oppressing you, sound a blast on the trumpets. Then you will be remembered by the Lord your God and rescued from your enemies."*

(Numbers 10:2, 9)

Whatever happened to the silver trumpets? If each church has made its own trumpet and developed its own distinctive sound, how can it be that your trumpet sounds off, and it doesn't alarm me though we are neighboring churches? I'm afraid to say that, though the trumpet blares, only a few are trained to respond to it. We are many individual churches with different methods, doctrines and people. However, there must be a particular blaring of the trumpet which causes us to lay aside the boundaries set by church membership and merge with the whole body of Christ in a united front against the enemy. If we don't learn to fight together, we will pass on a pattern of defeat to the next generation.

Chapter Eleven

WHAT IS "THE TRUTH BEHIND HIP HOP?" ADDRESSING THE CONTROVERSIAL DVD

*T*he *Truth Behind Hip Hop* by Minister G. Craige Lewis is a Christian video about the dangers of hip hop music. It has, for the most part, defined much of the church's understanding of hip hop culture. The DVD is several years old, but many churches still often refer to his teaching as a resource. If you are looking to understand Hip Hop culture, the teaching Minister Lewis includes is truly instrumental. Before you can effectively minister to any particular group of people, you need to know and understand the root of the culture's views and lifestyle. One would be a fool to take a missionary trip to Haiti and not study the influence of voodoo in that society. However, although the insight and research he gives in the DVD is exceptional, I do disagree with him in some areas. I am not trying to create discord, division, or even discredit this work. I simply want to offer insight and a different perspective in how we can approach hip hop culture. I pray that we as church leaders and the body of Christ are reminded that Paul said,

"Make every effort to keep the unity of the Spirit through the bond of peace." (Ephesians 4:3)

My greatest concern is that the church, after watching Lewis' video, is still left in the dark as to how to witness and evangelize to hip hop culture. *The Truth Behind Hip Hop* was a warning to the church to protect it against compromise, to guard against the subtle devices of the devil, and to maintain a perpetual standard of holiness. It gives revelation on how to protect the church from the dangers of Hip Hop by preaching a total separation from the culture. Lewis' purpose may not have been to discourage evangelism; however, his strong stance against the culture allowed churches to justify their unwillingness to step out into that mission field. What I want to do in this chapter is highlight specific areas in which I strongly disagree. It is impossible to evangelize without contact. Although the church needs to understand the evils of the culture, we need to take this information and use it as a tool for evangelism as opposed to separation.

A Beat is a Beat is a Beat, or Not

One topic that stemmed from Lewis' video is the controversy around using secular beats to produce Christian songs, such as Kirk Franklin has been doing for years. Some say you should not use secular beats because they have been conjured up by evil, demonic spirits. Others say that a beat is exactly that – just a beat. They argue that it doesn't matter if the beat was secular in its origin; if the words are of God, the beat can be used. Here's my take on it. Let's say that Snoop Dogg released a song that was hot about a year ago, and a Christian artist comes along later and wants to use the same beat. That is a no, no. When the song is played, we as the listening audience, Christian or not, will inevitably make comparisons with what Snoop created and what the Christian artist is doing with his song. Notice that I said with "his" song because what we are thinking is, 'Oh yeah, that's Snoop's song!' Trust me; it's not as easy to get to God when we are forced to push Snoop out of the way. Snoop just put the song out; it still belongs to him. The audience knows the song by heart. After all, it did sell two million copies. Remember what Paul told us, " 'Everything is permissible'- but not everything is beneficial. 'Everything is permissible'-but not everything is constructive." (1 Corinthians 10:23) In a case like this, your liberty in using Snoop's beat is the very thing that may confine or restrain the gospel.

Another instance when a secular beat should not be used is when it comes from a song that was originally filled with obscenities or foul language. Using a beat from a song that was plagued by all types of cursing is especially problematic because the non-Christian audience you are trying to reach knows where every curse word is. Hearing the beat just brings that all back to their mind. "…Make up your mind not to put any stumbling block or obstacle in your brother's way." (Romans 14:13) Remember, the prince of the power of the air is making every attempt to snatch the seed as every word is being planted. Our minds should not be filled with remembrance of the curse words that were in the original song.

Kirk Franklin's music became popular because he was using beats by secular artists; however, the songs he mimicked were 20 to 30 years old. That, in itself, is a very important factor that we don't consider. First of all, his use of secular beats isn't as offensive because he doesn't use songs that were originally full of curse words. Much of the music which was manufactured years ago would be considered as "good" and even non-offensive music now. Second, my mom may say, 'I don't really like his music because it reminds me of my partying days; it's too nostalgic.'

The youth of today may hear the music, like it, and not make the same connection because they are years removed from the time the song came out. They may know that it originated from an old song but wouldn't even know the original artist. They don't have any emotional ties to the song so they're able to accept and enjoy it as Christian music. The melody represents Christ to them, not an old school jam from back in the day. Nothing "…is unclean in itself. But if anyone regards something as unclean, then for him it is unclean." (Romans 14:14) Keeping this in mind, I don't ram that music down my mother's throat. Some of those songs may be connected to an old boyfriend of hers or may have been the major party theme in her day. Since it doesn't represent that for me, she doesn't judge me for listening to it.

When Christian artists use their own original beats that have a hip hop feel or sound, this is definitely OK. Some believe that gospel music should be locked into a particular sound, and if it doesn't sound like what they are accustomed to, we won't accept it as godly. I'm sure that how we worship now and how King David did in his time are two totally different styles. Jesus is not locked on the inside of an organ or choir robes. Why is it considered so offensive or wrong if gospel music creates a hip hop sound that can reach out to a hip hop audience? What exactly is a "church" sound?! Rick Warren made a great point in his book *A Purpose Driven Church* when he said,

> *"Songs that we now consider sacred classics were once as criticized as today's contemporary Christian music. When 'Silent Night' was first published, George Weber, music director of the Mainz Cathedral, called it 'vulgar mischief and void of all religious and Christian feelings.' "*[1]

The African American church doesn't have to reach back far into its music history to hear the influence of blues music, especially when listening to African American gospel quartets. The fact that many of our black churches do not accept rap as a form of "gospel" music presents the same issue that many white churches had to deal with in rock music. However, today, many of the Christian artists that are popular with white audiences, such as Third Day, Casting Crowns, Jars of Clay, Big Daddy Weave and Mercy Me, all have a rock foundation in terms of their music. When we hear it, we don't think of rock music; we think of Christian music. Will Christian rap reach this apex? I guess we will see.

Christian Rap: Is there such a thing?

Minister Lewis raised another issue which put the traditional church and those who are called to connect with hip hop culture in a divisive uproar. He says that there is no such thing as holy hip hop and that hip hop was defined by old school rappers as "booty shake," describing the dance styles of early hip hop audiences. Therefore, as Mr. Lewis puts it, holy hip hop would be defined as holy booty shaking which is disrespectful to God and Christians alike.

To be absolutely honest I don't totally disagree with Minister Lewis. I do agree that the origins of hip hop are anti-God. I also believe that it is impossible for two to walk together unless they agree, and the devil and God don't agree on anything. However there is a flip side to this. Jesus clearly told his disciples that they were in the world but not of it. Take for example a group of guys that hang out on the weekends and love to ride their motorcycles together. They wear the leather, the Harley jackets, and hang out in packs. Everywhere they go, they are identified as bikers. Because of groups like Hell's Angels or the Outlaws, bikers tend to have a negative reputation. These bikers, however, are Christians who claim Jesus as their Lord and Savior. Although in outward appearance they are just like any other biker, a closer look at their lifestyle, speech, and behavior would show their strong Christian standards. The same thing goes for Christian rock. Rock is what they identify with and what they are called to. Being a Christian defines who they are and whose they are. As discussed previously, rock has been accepted into the world of contemporary Christian music. If these groups have been accepted as having the capacity to be holy, why can't we embrace a Christian rapper as legitimately Godly? Just because the term holy hip hop is used in defining what they do doesn't mean that they yield themselves to every god hip hop offers. There is a plethora of Christian artists who do exceptional music offering solid doctrine and spiritual truths; they just happen to be rappers. These artists take an uncompromising stand in producing their music. One of the most respected and sought after Christian rap artists of today, Lecrae, has a song called "Go Hard." In it, he articulates his determination and passion to live his life 100% sold out for Jesus Christ. He literally asks God to kill him if he doesn't fulfill his mission and purpose of preaching the Gospel. He confronts his listeners with the question of whether others can tell they are Christians by the way they act. Lecrae actually challenges his audience to take on the same boldness for Christ as Paul had when he said, "...woe to me if I do not preach the gospel!" (1 Corinthians 9:16) This is only one example of the many exceptional songs by Christian rap artists that displays their true commitment and zeal to God and their Christian faith.

Regardless of whether this music is called holy hip hop, Christian rap or any other label, there's no doubt that Christians can have a place in the hip hop community and take a strong stand for Christ. In fact, accepting Christian rap in our churches and homes offers our young people an alternative that they can relate to. Unfortunately, when Mr. Lewis taught that there is no such thing as holy hip hop, it indirectly caused the church to close its doors to the potential positive influence that Christian rap could have on our youth.

Christian and Secular Sharing the Same Stage

Another issue that was raised on *The Truth Behind Hip Hop* DVD is the fact that T.D. Jakes invites some secular artists to perform at his annual MegaFest convention. Artists such as Patti Labelle, India Arie, and even Steve Harvey have performed as part of the entertainment portion at MegaFest, or "MegaMess" as Minister Lewis refers to it in his DVD. What does it say about the church when it promotes, sets the stage for, and even partners up with the world around it? I've been to MegaFest, and there is nothing like it in the world. To actually see the entire city of Atlanta taken over for a Christian convention is absolutely unbelievable! All the stores, hotels, and restaurants – the whole city caters to the Christian cause. The convention pours out to the city, attracting the Christian and the non-Christian alike. This event, to me, is an example of outreach at its highest degree. MegaFest drew approximately 100,000 people in its first year! Why is it that when we mix with the world, it is always looked at as if the world is going to suck us in instead of us pulling them out? Why couldn't a Steve Harvey diehard or a Patti Label loyalist expect to see their favorite artist but also meet Christ in the process? These performers draw an audience who would not normally come to an all-Christian event. This doesn't set the stage for a Steve Harvey. It does set the stage for salvation to the unbeliever. MegaFest makes it easy to evangelize an entire city that is in dire need of Christ.

I know that we would feel more comfortable if these stars were taking the stage as Spirit-filled believers, but that's not the case. Sometimes superstars, just as anyone else, search for Christ privately. Placing them on stage in front of the multitudes may start the salvation process for them. Very few Christian leaders can take these artists and put them on a stage that even they are humbled by. If we are going to influence the world with the gospel of Jesus Christ we need to deal with the people who entertain the masses, the kings and queens of the culture. To make my point a little clearer, I must refer to the story of Zacchaeus. The Bible tells us that,

> *"Jesus entered Jericho and was passing through. A man was there by the name of Zacchaeus; he was a chief tax collector and was wealthy. He wanted to see who Jesus was, but being a short man he could not, because of the crowd. So he ran ahead and climbed a sycamore-fig tree to see him, since Jesus was coming that way. When Jesus reached the spot, he looked up and said to him, 'Zacchaeus, come down immediately. I must stay at your house today.' So he came down at once and welcomed him gladly. All the people saw this and began to mutter, 'He has gone to be the guest of a 'sinner.' "* (Luke 19:1-7)

Zacchaeus was a rich tax collector and a man of great influence during his time. Jesus calls him out before he is actually saved and puts him "on stage" in front of the multitudes. He does become saved later in the text, but look where it started! We, like those of Zacchaeus' day, may question in our hearts or ponder in our minds what happens when Christians "mix" with secular artists, but let's be careful before we criticize. The question is not whether it looks right; the question is, 'Is it Christ-like?'

Dressed to Witness or Dressed to Support

After watching *The Truth Behind Hip Hop* DVD, a friend of mine asked me, "Rick, how do you feel about wearing gear from a clothing line owned by rappers who, in many ways, promote and finance their ungodly messages and agenda?" As ambassadors, the key to our mission is getting to the negotiating table. If wearing traditional Indian headgear and doing a customary tribal dance was a requirement for me to get in to witness to a particular tribal chief, that's exactly what I would do. My agenda from Christ as an ambassador supersedes any agenda for wearing the headgear or doing the dance, whether it is a custom or a tradition. The objective is getting into the chief's presence so that the village is saved. The principle doesn't change just because Hip Hop may be your friend, co-worker, or nephew. Scripture says,

> *"How, then, can they call on the one they have not believed in? And how can they believe in the one of whom they have not heard? And how can they hear without someone preaching to them?"* (Romans 10:14)

If I have to carry the gospel of Jesus Christ in a Sean John jumpsuit or walk in Sean Carter sneakers and wear a Phat Farm hat so that others can be saved, why not? How can they believe in whom they have not heard? In many cases, if you're not wearing the Sean John, they won't get close enough to hear your gospel. Remember, the woman at the well thought that all was normal at the well when she approached to get water. If something doesn't look normal or common to those we are witnessing to, they will create distance. We have been called ambassadors, but where is our tact and diplomacy? We're trying to dictate and tell them how they should feel and how to accept us on our terms. That's never an effective strategy, especially since we are also called to be servants.

"Your attitude should be the same as that of Christ Jesus: Who, being in very nature God, did not consider equality with God something to be grasped, but made himself nothing, taking the very nature of a servant, being made in human likeness." (Philippians 2:5)

Have we forgotten that Jesus wrapped himself up in sinful flesh and walked this earth for 33 years so he could get close enough to give us a gospel that would save our souls? Not only did He take on a fleshly body, but the God of all Heaven and earth came as an average Joe, a carpenter, for thirty years before he started His ministry. Many have disputed why Jesus' life as a child is not really addressed in the Bible. Maybe there simply wasn't much to write about, and that's what makes it glorious! He blended right in as a common Jew. If a Holy God can take on human flesh to bring about salvation, surely He doesn't have a problem with us wearing popular names and labels when the motive is evangelism. Instead of creating negotiating tables, even in how we dress, we're getting lazy, cold and indifferent in our efforts to deal with cultures unlike our own. "...I have become all things to all men so that by all possible means I might save some. I do all this for the sake of the gospel..." (1 Corinthians 9:22-23)

**A quick caution – a believer must research any symbol or artist's picture that may appear on clothing before wearing it. There are many symbols and images that have deeper meanings than can be seen on the surface. As Christians, we must be careful not to promote these unknowingly.

Chapter Twelve

LOVE, BUT NO LOVE SONGS

I cannot end this book without addressing one more issue that I feel is vital when considering our approach to hip hop culture. A natural human process in life is romantic love in relationships. Most everybody in the world experiences it at some point. It is truly a tragedy that we as Christians don't take advantage to minister through song what love between a man and a woman truly means. We don't, on a large scale, create, promote or endorse true, genuine love songs. Love is such a natural part of our existence and such a common topic, but we just don't have many Christian songs ministering in that area. I'm not saying we don't have *any* Christian love songs, but let's be honest – can you even name ten love songs originally written by Christian artists? I don't mean love songs to Jesus; I mean songs about love between a husband and wife. Even the ones you do know probably aren't on the top of your list. Often, our favorite love songs are by worldly artists. However, we get stuck when trying to decide if church folks will be offended by the selection of music at our wedding or cookout because it doesn't fit into the praise and worship category.

This topic was especially sensitive to me when I was engaged to my wife Christine. We both love the Lord and are mature Christians. She's been saved most of her life, teaches high school, has done several years of missionary work in Honduras, sings on praise and worship teams, and has led numerous discipleship classes in her church – a very disciplined Christian, to say the least. To give you an understanding of how disciplined she actually is, my nickname for her is "Rock" – imagine that! We often wanted to express our feelings for each other in the form of a song. We may have been out on a date, on our way to a nice restaurant, wanting to find a song that would help set the romantic tone for our evening. Needless to say, we rarely found that song on a Christian station. So we surfed the stations and ended up finding what we were looking for on a secular station. We love the song, but of course, we could never purchase the entire CD by that artist because that one good love song is the last track on the bottom of a heap of junk and filth. New to the love and relationship scene, I'm realizing how much help music can be in explaining some of the most difficult circumstances, helping me articulate what I want to say when I don't really know how. At one point in our engagement, Christine and I were having difficulty relating, and I can honestly say that much of that was because of me. After doing six years in prison and getting out so focused on ministry, I honestly didn't know how to open up and relate the love that I had for her. I had lost my touch; my rap was rusty after all those years of fellowship with the brothers! I was treating our relationship like ministry – approaching her as Minister Ricardo, not just Rick. I was having problems being vulnerable, intimate, and trusting, and we were struggling terribly as a result. Then, I heard a song at work by the secular artist Musiq Soulchild called "Teach Me." In it he speaks of how he was taught to be a man who never cries and works hard to provide for his family, a man who is strong and doesn't let anyone get too close. The chorus of the song is a plea to his girl asking her to teach him how to open himself up and love freely. When I heard the song, I was like, "Man, that's me; that's me, that's my song!" A few days later, when Christine and I were riding in the car, the song came on the radio. I simply turned it up, and she listened. She smiled, and I knew she understood. It had worked like a charm. I was "the man" again, just as cool as a cucumber. Christian or not, we men especially go through phases such as these. We've either never been committed and have conditioned ourselves to be impersonal or we aren't even aware of it until the woman has issues. How amazing it would be if songs such as these were on Christian CD's! Love will always be an area available for us to minister to an unsaved world. We're the ones who are supposed to have the revelation – the key to how to love our partners in sincerity and truth. A love song is a great open door to minister to couples; yet, it's a door we seldom open. We've given the devil free reign to teach an entire generation what standards to set in a relationship and what to expect. Of course, his message is full of sex, selfishness and broken hearts. We give secular artists too much room to minister about common issues everybody goes through, and love is one of them. And we wonder why love and relationships often become lust and promiscuity!

OUT

Hip Hop and the church – this is not a new phenomenon. With the success of artists such as Kirk Franklin and Toby Mac, hip hop styles and trends are becoming more of the norm and are at least tolerated in our churches, if not embraced. For some, Hip Hop will always be the soundtrack which choreographs the moves of a teenage horror film filled with violence, drugs and promiscuity or the sonic boom that screams from candy-coated chariots sitting on 22-inch rims at every red light. To say the least this is still a touchy subject for the church, almost as divisive as the presidential campaign between Obama and McCain. Left, right, young, old, conservative, contemporary – subjects such as music and entertainment force us to pick a side and vehemently state our case. I am concerned that, in many instances, we are so passionate about articulating our theological position on the controversy that our desire to formulate the "correct" argument has taken precedence over all else. We, therefore, speak of Hip Hop as a subject or a thing and forget that real people are trapped inside this great debate, confined by our disunity and disagreement. When two elephants rumble in the jungle, it is the jungle which suffers the most damage. We've debated; we've been briefed; now, will we go?

We all know that Jonah ran the other way when God called him to Nineveh. He didn't run simply because he was afraid. He did so because he didn't want to be the mouthpiece of mercy and grace to an evil, gentile nation that, according to him, was undeserving. Once Jonah reluctantly became obedient to God and preached repentance, the people of Nineveh responded by fasting and turning from their evil ways. As a result, God did not bring destruction on their city. Jonah voiced his anger at God by saying,

> *"O Lord, is this not what I said when I was still at home? That is why I was so quick to flee to Tarshish. I knew that you are a gracious and compassionate God, slow to anger and abounding in love, a God who relents from sending calamity."* (Jonah 4:2)

Jonah was furious because God had had mercy on the wicked. He then said, "Now, O LORD, take away my life, for it is better for me to die than to live." (Jonah 4:3) How could Jonah be so selfish? Yet, many Christians secretly harbor this same resentment. It's amazing how we can feel like we have God's grace and mercy at our disposal, as if we can hide it from whom we choose and do with it as we please! We call ourselves Christians and have the audacity to decide for God who is deserving of His mercy and who is not.

> *"All this is from God, who reconciled us to himself through Christ and gave us the ministry of reconciliation: that God was reconciling the world to himself in Christ, not counting men's sins against them. And he has committed to us the message of reconciliation. We are therefore*

124

Christ's ambassadors, as though God were making his appeal through us. " (2 Corinthians 5:18-20)

It is not God's will that any man perish, not even the guy with the foul mouth, tattoos and gold teeth. Our lack of compassion for hip hop culture is a greater hindrance to their salvation than their own sinful ways.

Jesus didn't come to me by way of a preacher in a pulpit, but through a fellow inmate—one who understood my language, my situation, my issues and my past. My own conversion is a testament of how Jesus can intervene, interrupt and create dialogue within the confines of a hip hop community in order to bring about salvation. I never knew that Jesus would become a prisoner so that I could be made free. Having now received salvation, I desire to find a way to communicate God's message of love and grace to people who, like me, find themselves in a pit of shame and despair. I hope to motivate pastors, ministers, leaders, parents and lay people to confidently step into hip hop culture with the love and compassion of Jesus Christ.

Notes

Chapter One

1. *Get Rich or Die Tryin'*, DVD, directed by Jim Sheridan (2005; Hollywood, CA: Paramount Pictures, 2006).
2. Ethan Brown, *Queens Reigns Supreme: Fat Cat, 50 Cent and the Rise of the Hip Hop Hustler* (New York, Random House Inc., 2005), xxi.

Chapter Two

1. Tupac Shakur and others, *Tupac: Resurrection 1971–1996* (New York, Simon and Schuster, 2003), 54.
2. Michael Eric Dyson, *Holler If You Hear Me: Searching for Tupac Shakur* (New York, Basic Civitas Books, 2002), 212.
3. "Tupac's quotes," *Thugz Network*, http://www.thugz-network.com/Tupac~Shakur~Quotes.php.
4. Tupac Shakur, *The Rose That Grew from Concrete* (New York, Simon and Schuster, 1999), 150.
5. Tupac Shakur and others, *Tupac: Resurrection 1971–1996* (New York, Simon and Schuster, 2003), 121.
6. Vibe Magazine and Quincy Jones, *Tupac Shakur, 1971-1996* (New York, Three Rivers Press, 1997), 98.

Chapter Five

1. imprecate. Dictionary.com. *The American Heritage® Dictionary of the English Language, Fourth Edition.* Houghton Mifflin Company, 2004. http://dictionary.reference.com/browse/imprecate (accessed: February 05, 2010).

Chapter Seven

1. 50 Cent and Kris Ex, *From Pieces to Weight: Once upon a time in Southside, Queens* (New York, Simon and Schuster, 2005), 198.
2. Ibid., 212.

Chapter Ten

1. Rick Warren, *The Purpose Driven Church* (Grand Rapids, Zondervan, 1995), 283.

CPSIA information can be obtained
at www.ICGtesting.com
Printed in the USA
BVHW032013240519
549109BV00005B/124/P